MW00559130

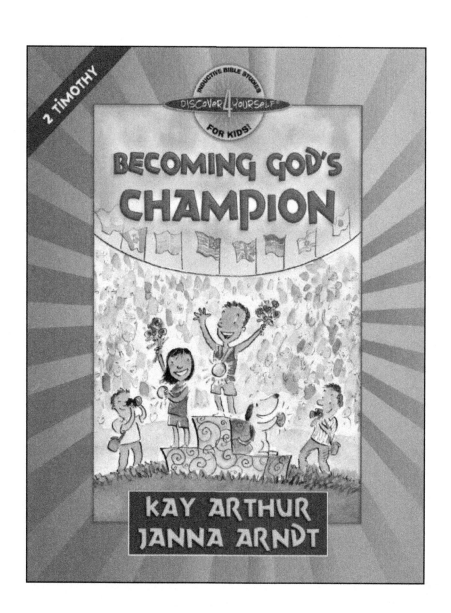

TEACHER GUIDE

Elizabeth A. McAllister, Ed. D.

BECOMING GOD'S CHAMPION TEACHER GUIDE
Published by Precept Ministries of Reach Out, Inc.
P. O. Box 182218
Chattanooga, TN 37422

ISBN 978-1-62119-043-1

All Scripture quotations, unless otherwise indicated, are taken from the *NEW AMERICAN STANDARD BIBLE*® (NASB)
© Copyright 1960, 1962, 1963, 1968, 1971, 1972, 1973, 1975, 1977, 1995 by the. Used by permission. (www.lockman.org)

D4Y Teacher Guides were made possible by the generous gift of a long-time friend of Precept Ministries.

Author Photo and Cover by John Phillips

Graphics Design by Michele Walker

Copyright © 2014 Precept Ministries International

All rights reserved. No part of this publication may be reproduced or transmitted in any form or by any means electronic or mechanical, including photocopying and recording, or by any information storage and retrieval system, without the prior written permission of the publisher.

Printed in the United States of America

Precept, Precept Ministries International, Precept Ministries International the Inductive Bible Study People, the Plumb Bob design, Precept Upon Precept, In & Out, Sweeter than Chocolate!, Cookies on the Lower Shelf, Precepts For Life, Precepts From God's Word and Transform Student Ministries are trademarks of Precept Ministries International.

BECOMING GOD'S CHAMPION

TEACHER GUIDE
TABLE OF CONTENTS

BECOMING GOD'S CHAMPION
TEACHER GUIDE

Introduction

Thank you for selecting this Bible study for your child and/or class. Leading children to read, observe, interpret, and apply the Bible for themselves offers them a bridge from hearsay to real truth. As they learn to be comfortable with the idea that they can read the Bible, they will take the task seriously.

The Discover 4 Yourself series is designed to lead young students through the process of inductive study: question, question, question, search, think, understand, and apply. They will be comfortable with this process only after you prove that the possibility is within their reach.

BECOMING GOD'S CHAMPION is a study of 2 Timothy. You will discover a letter Paul wrote to Timothy while he was in prison. Paul encourages Timothy to stay faithful and run the race to the finish line during a time when many people were turning away from the true Gospel.

To prepare to lead **BECOMING GOD'S CHAMPION** work through each "Day" on your own before consulting the Teacher Guide. Since this is an Inductive Bible Study, your teaching will be more effective if you do the work first and God reveals His truth to you.

Whether you're homeschooling a child, teaching a Sunday school class, teaching in a Christian school, or simply using these studies for your child's quiet time or family Bible study, this Teacher Guide will show you how to clearly and carefully lead each child through Inductive Bible study. We offer suggestions to guide you step-by-step. *Instructional Strategies* explains why certain activities are used throughout the book. Choose the activities that best fit your situation.

Homeschooling Parents and Family Bible Study

We suggest you do one "Day" per day unless it's too much for your child's reading and/or writing skills. You can work with your child and discuss what you learn together or let him/her work independently, saving discussion times for later.

You may want to join or create a homeschool group that meets once a week to do these studies. The teacher will assign a week of homework in class. The following week the teacher will lead the students to discuss what they discovered, how to apply it, and to work on any creative elements included in the study or play a game to review what they have learned.

Sunday School Teachers

To use these studies in a weekly Sunday school class we suggest you do one "Day" together with your children each week in class, since you will have children from different backgrounds, even some from families that are not members of or even regularly attend a church.

Each Sunday briefly review the prior Sunday's work to put them in context for the next day of study in their book. After completing a week in the book you may want to have a "Game Time Sunday" to review the material before you move on to the next week. Game time makes learning fun for children and shows you the extent to which they understand what they learned.

You can keep the books at church and have the children take home verses on index cards or pieces of paper to memorize.

Classroom Teachers

Generally, classroom teachers face many different learning abilities within their groups. It is important for you to understand these different learning abilities so that you can meet each child where he or she is so that no one is left behind during the process.

It is important for you to bring in *schemata* (background information) for students to draw on. If you tie studies to something children already know, they will grasp the lessons clearly.

Grasp is also affected by *metacognition*—the ability to monitor understanding of the text. Students must be able to perform several functions to develop metacognitive control over reading and understanding. He or she must be able to:

1. Ask first, "What do I already know about this topic?" then, "Do I have enough information to understand this text?" Answers to these questions will directly influence the use of the inductive method.

2. Identify the purpose for reading each selection.

3. Focus on particular information.

4. Monitor understanding by recalling background knowledge and relating it to the context by asking questions like: "How am I doing?" "Am I keeping the big picture in mind?" "Am I bogged down?" "If so, how do I fix it—reread the passages or ask for help?" (Nothing wrong with the latter.)

5. Evaluate understanding of the context by asking, "What did I learn?" With respect to Inductive Bible Study, "How do I apply this information?"

Instructional Strategies

Writing as a response reinforces learning and so this method is prevalent in these books. Encourage students to share ideas and insights with you and other students.

Reading is the highest intellectual activity of the human experience. More sectors of the brain are active than in other endeavors including mathematics and flying an airplane. It's the most totally interactive processing of information, even when children are reading Mother Goose.

Take time for students to read aloud with a friend. Reading *out loud* and listening promote interactions between the brain's left and right hemispheres and activate little-used pathways. Reading *silently* activates a much smaller part of the brain.

Give students a chance to express themselves at every opportunity. This forces them to retrieve information stored in their *schemata* (background knowledge) for application to new information. What better opportunity is there than to *inductively* look at curriculum and context?

You will notice that you are asked to read some content aloud (as) students follow along. This frees unsure readers to focus on context rather than decoding strategies. By doing this, you will remove stumbling blocks to understanding; otherwise, reluctant readers will be convinced that inductive study is impossible for them—the last thought you want to instill!

We have included weekly quizzes with memory verses and also multiple-choice questions that will force students to think about what they have learned. Based on how they answer these questions, you will know whether they have grasped the material adequately.

In view of this sparse introduction to learning requirements for success, it's important that you apply strategies that lead students to develop the ability to self-monitor understanding of context each step of the way. These **Teacher Guides** offer suggestions to assure that students, regardless of their abilities, will learn to read the Bible with understanding as you lead them, step-by-step, through the Inductive Study Method.

Discover 4 Yourself Objectives

The Discover 4 Yourself series objectives are not the same as the behavioral objectives of general subject matter. The books contain outstanding biblical subjects of course, but they are written *primarily* to be a tool for young students to learn the Inductive Bible Study Method.

Playing an instrument well requires repetition and application of skills learned. Similarly, effective study is developed by repeated practice and good role modeling of an outstanding study method. Accordingly these **Teacher Guides** contain global objectives for the student *and the teacher*.

We'll start with the teacher.

Discover 4 Yourself Teacher Guide Objectives

✓ To help the teacher identify students' metacognitive needs as they read texts.

✓ To show the teacher how to model use of the Inductive Study Method so students will be able to apply the techniques independently when studying God's Word.

✓ To offer the teacher effective teaching strategies to assure that students succeed when they study the Bible.

Discover 4 Yourself Student Workbook Objectives

✓ To learn how to read, observe, and interpret the Bible for themselves.

✓ To practice this method independently within an encouraging environment.

Scripture quotations in this book are taken from the New American Standard Bible ®, © 1960, 1962, 1963, 1968, 1971, 1972, 1973, 1975, 1977, 1995 by The Lockman Foundation. Used by permission. (www.Lockman.org)

DISCOVER 4 YOURSELF is a registered trademark of The Hawkins Children's LLC. Harvest House Publishers, Inc., is the exclusive licensee of the federally registered trademark DISCOVER 4 YOURSELF.

Illustrations © by Steve Bjorkman

Cover by Left Coast Design, Portland, Oregon

Discover 4 Yourself® Inductive Bible Studies for Kids
BECOMING GOD'S CHAMPION

Copyright © 2009 by Precept Ministries International
Published by Harvest House Publishers
Eugene, Oregon 97402
www.harvesthousepublishers.com

ISBN 978-0-7369-2594-5

All rights reserved. No part of this publication may be reproduced, stored in a retrieval system, or transmitted in any form or by any means—electronic, mechanical, digital, photocopy, recording, or any other—except for brief quotations in printed reviews, without the prior permission of the publisher.

Printed in the United States of America

13 14 15 16 17 18 19 20 / ML-SK / 10 9 8 7 6 5 4 3 2

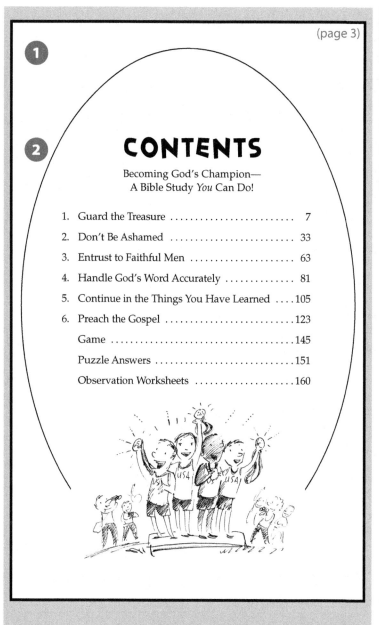

(page 3)

CONTENTS

Becoming God's Champion—
A Bible Study *You* Can Do!

Guided Instruction

1 Give a copy of *Becoming God's Champion* to each student.

2 Together, turn to the CONTENTS page. Lead students through a quick overview of the book. Point out the structure of each chapter, noting that there will be a lesson and activities to do each day for five days.

"Guard the Treasure" **7**

Molly and Max are in a summer camp to train to be true champions for God. They will begin by learning about different types of literature in the Bible. The book of 2 Timothy is a letter in the New Testament. Paul has written this personal letter to Timothy, his son in the faith, to warn him about the dangers of being too lazy when handling the Word of God. He warns Timothy to guard the treasure entrusted to him.

"Don't be Ashamed" **33**

You will watch Paul remind Timothy to kindle the gift of God so his faith will blaze to others. Timothy has everything he needs to be a champion for God. God has given him power, love, and a sound mind through Jesus Christ. You will observe the instructions Paul shared with Timothy so that he will stay on track.

"Entrust to Faithful Men" **63**

Paul reminds Timothy about the hardships he suffers for the Word of God. He encourages him to remain faithful and to remind fellow believers that they are responsible to continue to share the Gospel with others. They may experience hardships but they must endure and hold Christ's banner high enough for everyone to see.

"Handle God's Word Accurately" **81**

It is an awesome privilege to handle God's Word. We need to study it carefully so we have the message correct when we share it with others. We don't want to change it in any way. God's Word is exact—He means every word He says exactly as He gave it.

"Continue in the Things You Have Learned" **105**

Though we are to handle God's Word accurately, we are also to be vessels of honor for God to use us. We need to correct those who oppose us gently with the Word so they will repent and turn to the truth. Leading someone to turn around and embrace Jesus Christ is an awesome responsibility and privilege.

"Preach the Gospel" **123**

Paul continues to remind Timothy of the importance of knowing God's Word and about the need to lead others to Jesus Christ. Paul warns Timothy that some will turn away from the truth but he encourages him to remain sober, endure hardships, and work as an evangelist to fulfill his ministry.

3 After leading students through an overview of the Contents, turn to "Becoming God's Champion" on page 5 and read the introduction to your students.

Guided Instruction

(page 5)

3

BECOMING GOD'S CHAMPION— A BIBLE STUDY YOU CAN DO!

Hey guys, guess what? Molly, Sam (the great, face-licking detective beagle), and I are getting ready for a great new Bible adventure. By the way, my name is Max, and we want you to join us as we go to a summer sports camp to train to become champions for God. Doesn't that sound exciting?

While we are at camp competing in our summer games, we are also going to look at our official Rulebook, the Bible, to learn about a letter that one of God's champions wrote to his son in the faith. WHO wrote this awesome letter that shows us how to be a champion for God? WHAT is the good news about Jesus Christ? Have you believed it? WHOM are you going to pass the baton, the good news about Jesus Christ, on to? HOW are you going to stay faithful and run the race when others quit and turn away? And WHY is it so important for you to know God's Word for yourself?

You'll get the answers to all these questions and win the race that God has set for you, as you study the Bible, the source of all truth, and ask God's Spirit to lead and guide you. Psalm 119:102 shows us that God is the one who teaches us. Isn't that cool? God is our Coach!

You also have this book, which is an inductive Bible study. The word *inductive* means you go straight to the Bible *yourself* to investigate what the book of 2 Timothy shows you about guarding the gospel and entrusting it to others. In inductive Bible study, you discover 4 yourself what the Bible says and means.

Aren't you excited? Grab your official Rulebook and get ready for an *awesome* summer as you train to become God's champion by knowing His Word so you can pass the baton to others, finish the course, and receive a crown that will last forever!

THINGS YOU'LL NEED

New American Standard Bible (updated edition)—preferably the *New Inductive Study Bible* (NISB) Have you gotten yours yet?

Pen or pencil   A dictionary

Colored pencils   This workbook

Index cards

1

GUARD THE TREASURE

④ ## 2 TIMOTHY 1–4

"Hey guys!" Max called out. "Welcome to summer sports camp! Aren't you excited? You're going to get to compete in the same kind of games that they have in the Olympics. We're going to train to be true champions for God. Why don't you head to your rooms and unpack. Then we'll meet you at Hardaway Hall to begin our training on becoming God's champion."

DAY ONE
EXERCISE YOUR MIND

"Great, you're here!" Molly called out. "Uh-oh, you better watch out. Sam is going to be pretty excited to have you here at our summer sports camp. He has been practicing and practicing his events since Uno the beagle won the best of breed at the Westminster dog show. Sam knows he is an awesome detective beagle, and now he wants to be a champion too! Oh no, it's too late—he sees you, so get ready for a good face licking."

"Wait, Sam!" Max yelled out. "Don't jump up on them!" Oops—too late. Sam sure gets excited when he sees you. Hurry

7

Guided Instruction

WEEK 1

DAY ONE

Ask God to meet you during this lesson to instill His Word in your heart.

④ Read the introduction "2 Timothy 1-4" and "Exercise Your Mind." Discuss the type of literature 2 Timothy is with your students and how to study a letter in the New Testament.

Guided Instruction

up and give him a treat so he'll get down and quit licking. All right, now that you're here and Sam is munching on his treat, we can get started on our first training exercise.

Molly smiled, "WHAT is the first thing you need to do before you get started? Do you remember? You've got it! P __ __ __!

"Remember, Bible study should always begin with prayer. We need to ask God to help us understand what the Bible says and to direct us by His Holy Spirit so we can make sure we understand His Word and handle it accurately."

Now that we've talked to God, our "heavenly Coach," and asked for His help, we are ready to do our first exercise to train our mind. Did you know that the Bible is made up of different kinds of literature? Some books in the Bible are historical, some are biographical, and others are poetic, proverbial, prophetic, epistles (letters), or a combination—like the book of Daniel, which is both a historical and a prophetic book. We are going to study the book of 2 Timothy, which is an epistle (a letter).

When we study a letter in the Bible, we do it differently than we would study a historical book. The first thing we need to do when we study any letter in the New Testament is to read the whole letter to find out WHO wrote the letter, to WHOM it was written, WHAT the letter is about, and WHY it was written.

When we read a letter today, sometimes we don't know who wrote the letter until we see the signature at the end. But in Bible times the writer of the letter identified himself immediately instead of waiting until the end of the letter. The letter was signed at the beginning!

Our first exercise is to read the letter to find out WHO wrote it and to WHOM it was written. Let's get started by reading 2 Timothy 1 and looking for the people.

Turn to your Observation Worksheets on page 160. Observation Worksheets have the Bible text printed out for you to use as you do your study on 2 Timothy.

Read 2 Timothy 1 and mark every reference to the author of the book (WHO wrote the letter) in a special way. Color him blue.

Mark every reference to the recipient (to WHOM it was written) by coloring him orange.

Guided Instruction

5 Discuss marking the author blue, the recipient orange, and any other names in pink (not including God or Jesus), and any pronouns for these people. Turn to page 160 and read 2 Timothy 1 aloud as students follow along. If you are teaching in a classroom and have an overhead projector, make a transparency of your Observation Worksheet for a visual aid. You may want to blow it up to poster size and hang it on a wall and then have your students call each key word out loud as you read it and mark it together—you on the transparency and they in their books. If you're skilled at PowerPoint and have time, you can import an Observation Worksheet then select symbols from PP's palette or elsewhere, color them, place them over the words, and even animate them—bring them in one at a time.

Guard the Treasure 9

Mark all of the other names (*not* including God or Jesus) by coloring them pink.

And don't forget to make sure you mark the pronouns that refer to the author, the recipient, and the other people, each in the right color.

What's a pronoun? Check out the Max and Molly's exercise manual below:

Pronouns

Pronouns are words that take the place of nouns. A noun is a person, place, or thing. A pronoun stands in for a noun! Here's an example: "Max is an awesome runner. He can't wait to compete on the relay team." The word *he* is a pronoun because it takes the place of Max's name in the second sentence. *He* is another word we use to refer to Max.

Watch for these other pronouns when you are marking people:

I, me, my, mine	it, its
you, your, yours	we, us, our, ours
he, him, his	she, her, hers
they, them, their, theirs	

(page 160)

OBSERVATION WORKSHEETS
2 TIMOTHY

5 Chapter 1

1 Paul, an apostle of Christ Jesus by the will of God, according to the promise of life in Christ Jesus,

2 To Timothy, my beloved son: Grace, mercy and peace from God the Father and Christ Jesus our Lord.

3 I thank God, whom I serve with a clear conscience the way my forefathers did, as I constantly remember you in my prayers night and day,

4 longing to see you, even as I recall your tears, so that I may be filled with joy.

5 For I am mindful of the sincere faith within you, which first dwelt in your grandmother Lois and your mother Eunice, and I am sure that it is in you as well.

Guided Instruction

am sure that it is in you as well.

6 For this reason I remind you to kindle afresh the gift of God which is in you through the laying on of my hands.

7 For God has not given us a spirit of timidity, but of power and love and discipline.

8 Therefore do not be ashamed of the testimony of our Lord or of me His prisoner, but join with me in suffering for the gospel according to the power of God,

9 who has saved us and called us with a holy calling, not according to our works, but according to His own purpose and grace which was granted us in Christ Jesus from all eternity,

10 but now has been revealed by the appearing of our Savior Christ Jesus, who abolished death and brought life and immortality to light through the gospel,

11 for which I was appointed a preacher and an apostle and a teacher.

160

12 For this reason I also suffer these things, but I am not ashamed; for I know whom I have believed and I am convinced that He is able to guard what I have entrusted to Him until that day.

13 Retain the standard of sound words which you have heard from me, in the faith and love which are in Christ Jesus.

14 Guard, through the Holy Spirit who dwells in us, the treasure which has been entrusted to you.

15 You are aware of the fact that all who are in Asia turned away from me, among whom are Phygelus and Hermogenes.

16 The Lord grant mercy to the house of Onesiphorus, for he often refreshed me and was not ashamed of my chains;

17 but when he was in Rome, he eagerly searched for me and found me—

18 the Lord grant to him to find mercy from the Lord on that day—and you know very well what services he rendered at Ephesus.

(page 9)

2 Timothy 1:1 WHO wrote this letter? <u>Paul</u>

2 Timothy 1:2 To WHOM was the letter written?
<u>Timothy</u>

Now that we have discovered that Paul wrote this letter to Timothy, let's find out WHAT we can learn about Paul. Look at every place you marked *Paul* by coloring him blue on your Observation Worksheet in 2 Timothy 1, and fill in the list in the box on the next page.

---

10   WEEK ONE

WHAT I Learned About Paul

2 Timothy 1:1 Paul is an <u>apostle</u> of <u>Christ Jesus</u>.

2 Timothy 1:3 Paul t <u>h a n k</u> s God.

2 Timothy 1:3 Paul s <u>e r v e</u> s God with a <u>clear conscience</u>. Paul p <u>r a y</u> s for Timothy.

2 Timothy 1:4 Paul l <u>o n g</u> s to <u>see</u> Timothy so that he will be filled with <u>joy</u>.

2 Timothy 1:8 Paul is the Lord's p <u>r i s o n e</u> r. Paul is <u>suffering</u> for the g <u>o s p e l</u>.

2 Timothy 1:11 Paul was appointed a <u>preacher</u> and an <u>apostle</u> and a <u>teacher</u> for the gospel.

2 Timothy 1:12 Paul s <u>u f f e r</u> s for the gospel. Paul is not a <u>s h a m e d</u> of the gospel. Paul is convinced that <u>he</u> is able to <u>guard</u> what he has <u>entrusted</u> to Him until that day.

2 Timothy 1:16-17 Paul is r <u>e f r e s h e d</u> by Onesiphorus. Paul is in c <u>h a i n s</u> in R <u>o m e</u>.

Guided Instruction

6 Reread the selected verses to answer the questions.

2 Timothy 1:1 WHO wrote this letter? <u>Paul</u>

2 Timothy 1:2 To WHOM was the letter written? <u>Timothy</u>

7 Fill in the blanks to complete "WHAT I Learned About Paul" on page 10.

WHAT I Learned About Paul

2 Timothy 1:1 Paul is an <u>apostle</u> **of** <u>Christ</u> <u>Jesus</u>.

2 Timothy 1:3 Paul t <u>h a n k</u> s **God.**

2 Timothy 1:3 Paul s <u>e r v e</u> s **God with a** <u>clear conscience</u>. **Paul** p <u>r a y</u> s **for Timothy.**

2 Timothy 1:4 Paul l <u>o n g</u> s **to** <u>see</u> **Timothy so that he will be filled with** <u>joy</u>.

2 Timothy 1:8 Paul is the Lord's p <u>r i s o n e</u> r. **Paul is** <u>suffering</u> **for the** g <u>o s p e l</u>.

2. Timothy 1:11 Paul was appointed a <u>preacher</u> **and an** <u>apostle</u> **and a** <u>teacher</u> **for the gospel.**

2 Timothy 1:12 Paul s <u>u f f e r</u> s **for the gospel. Paul is not a** <u>s h a m e d</u> **of the gospel. Paul is convinced that** <u>he</u> **is able to** <u>guard</u> **what he has** <u>entrusted</u> **to Him until that day.**

2 Timothy 1:16-17 Paul is r <u>e f r e s h e d</u> **by Onesiphorus. Paul is in** c <u>h a i n s</u> **in** R <u>o m e</u>.

Guided Instruction

 Lead a discussion about how students can serve God and then ask them to respond in writing on page 11.

WHAT do you see about Paul's circumstances in 2 Timothy 1:8, 16?

1:8   Paul is <u>suffering</u> for the g <u>o</u> <u>s</u> p <u>e</u> l.

He is the Lord's p <u>r</u> <u>i</u> <u>s</u> <u>o</u> <u>n</u> <u>e</u> r.

1:16 Paul is in c <u>h</u> <u>a</u> <u>i</u> <u>n</u> s.

Read the rest of the text and discuss the importance of context and answer the question on page 12.

(page 10)

8 Fantastic! Just look at what you have discovered by looking at one person in a small section of this letter. You discovered that Paul was an apostle, of Jesus Christ. That means he was a messenger of the good news about Jesus Christ. He was appointed a

---

Guard the Treasure 11

preacher, an apostle and a teacher. Paul is serving God by telling other people the good news about Jesus Christ.

HOW can you serve God? Write out one way that you

can serve God. _____

_____

Looking at your list, WHAT do you see about Paul's circumstances in 2 Timothy 1:8,16?

1:8 Paul is ____**suffering**____ for the g o s p e l.
He is the Lord's p r i s o n e r.

1:16 Paul is in c h a i n s.

Wow! It looks like Paul is in some pretty hard circumstances. He is in prison, suffering for the gospel. This question you just answered about Paul's circumstances gives us a chance to talk about something important called *context*.

Context is a combination of two words: *con*, which means "with," and *text*, which means "what is written." Context is the setting in which something is found. When you look for context in the Bible, you look at the verses surrounding the passage you are studying. Then you also think about where the passage fits in the big picture of the chapter you are studying, how it fits in the book, and then how it fits into the whole Bible.

Context also includes these:

- The place where something happens. (This is **geographical** context. WHERE is this happening? Is this taking place in Rome, Israel, or the United States?)

- The time in history when an event happens. (This is **historical** context. WHEN is this happening? Is it before Jesus died on the cross or after?)

- The customs of a group of people. (This is **cultural** context. WHAT did people in Bible times wear? Did they wear tunics or shorts and T-shirts?)

12   WEEK ONE

It's always important to be on the lookout for the context because it helps you discover WHAT the Bible is saying. WHAT do Paul's circumstances help you see about the time when Paul lived (the historical context)? Just from what you have seen today, do you think it was an easy time in history to be a Christian, or do you think Christians were persecuted and suffering during this time in history? Write out what you think on the line below.

_____

All right! Today we started getting the big picture of Paul's letter to Timothy, and we discovered that Paul is in prison, suffering for the gospel. We'll get the details later.

As we head outside to practice carrying the flags for the opening ceremony of our summer sports camp, look at the flags of the different countries we will represent here at camp.

Each flag has a number inside the ball at the top of the flagpole. Look at the number inside the ball and find the matching blank below. Write the word written on the flagpole on the correct blank to solve this week's verse. Then turn to 2 Timothy 1 and find the reference for this verse.

Guided Instruction

9 Solve the memory verse on page 13. Copy it to an index card and say it three times, three times a day.

Guard, through the Holy Spirit who dwells in us, the treasure which has been entrusted to you.

2 Timothy 1:4

Guard the Treasure   13

9 _____Guard_____, through the ___Holy___ ___Spirit___ who
          1   2   3

___dwells___ in ___us___, the ___treasure___ which has been
      4   5   6

___entrusted___ to ___you___.
        7   8

2 Timothy 1: _4_

Way to go! Now write this verse out and practice saying it three times in a row out loud today!

DAY TWO
REFUELING YOUR BODY

10

Good morning! Did you get a good night's sleep? You know it's very important for athletes to get eight to ten hours of sleep at night so their bodies can rest, recover, and restore their energy. Let's go through the breakfast line and get our food so we can fuel our bodies and get back to our training. Our minds and our muscles need a good breakfast so they will be ready to do some hard work to help us become true Olympians for God!

That was soooo good! We saw you feeding Sam a little bacon under the table. He is going to love you forever! Now that we have rested and refueled, we need to get back to the letter of 2 Timothy. Studying the Bible is the most important exercise we can ever do!

Today we are going to continue to get the big picture of our letter. Turn to page 160 and read 2 Timothy 1 again.

Now, look at every place where you marked *Timothy* in orange yesterday on your Observation Worksheet. In the box on the next page, make a list of what you learned about Timothy.

Guided Instruction

DAY TWO

Remember to bring God into your study of His Word. He will lead you to clear understanding.

10 Turn to page 14 and read "Refueling Your Body."

Guided Instruction

11 Make a list in the box on page 15 about Timothy.

WHAT I Learned About Timothy

2 Timothy 1:2 Timothy is Paul's underline{beloved son}.

2 Timothy 1:5 Timothy has a underline{sincere faith}, which he received from his underline{grandmother} L o i s and his underline{mother} E u n i c e.

2 Timothy 1:6 The g i f t of G o d is in Timothy.

2 Timothy 1:14 The underline{treasure} has been entrusted to Timothy.

Read the rest of the text on page 15 and review the 5W and H questions.

Guard the Treasure   15

11

WHAT I Learned About Timothy

2 Timothy 1:2 Timothy is Paul's ___beloved___ ___son___ .

2 Timothy 1:5 Timothy has a ___sincere___ ___faith___, which he received from his ___grandmother___ L o i s and his ___mother___ E u n i c e.

2 Timothy 1:6 The g i f t of G o d is in Timothy.

2 Timothy 1:14 The ___treasure___ has been entrusted to Timothy.

Isn't that awesome? Timothy is Paul's beloved son. That doesn't mean Paul was really Timothy's father; it means Timothy has a close relationship to Paul, like a father-son relationship. Timothy is Paul's son as a believer in Jesus. We see that Timothy has a sincere faith—that's a faith that is real! Timothy learned about faith from his mother and grandmother. And he has been entrusted with the gospel so he can share the good news about Jesus with others!

Look at the other people in 2 Timothy 1 that you colored pink. Let's ask the 5 W's and an H to get some details on these people. WHAT are the 5 W's and an H? They are the WHO, WHAT, WHERE, WHEN, WHY, and HOW questions.

1. Asking WHO helps you find out…

   WHO wrote this?

   WHOM are we reading about?

   WHOM was it written to?

   WHO said this or did that?

2. WHAT helps you understand…

16 WEEK ONE

WHAT the author is talking about.

WHAT are the main things that happen?

3. WHERE helps you learn…

WHERE something happened.

WHERE did they go?

WHERE was this said?

When we discover a "where," we double underline the "where" in green.

4. WHEN tells us about time. We mark it with a green clock 🕐 or a green circle like this: ○ .

WHEN tells us…

WHEN did this event happen? Or WHEN will it happen?

WHEN did the main characters do something? This helps us to follow the order of events.

5. WHY asks questions like…

WHY did he say that?

WHY did they go there?

WHY did this happen?

6. HOW lets you figure out things like…

HOW something is to be done.

HOW people knew something had happened.

Now, as you ask the 5 W's and an H about these other people, you are going to see a *contrast*. A contrast shows two things that are different or opposite, like light and dark.

Guided Instruction

Read the selected verses and answer the questions on pages 16-17.

Guided Instruction

2 Timothy 1:15 WHO are the people mentioned in this verse?

1. All who are in <u>Asia</u>

2. P<u>h y g e l u s</u>

3. H<u>e r m o g e n e s</u>

2 Timothy 1:15 WHAT did this group of people in Asia do? They <u>turned</u> <u>away</u> from Paul.

2 Timothy 1:16-18 WHO is the person mentioned in these verses? <u>Onesiphorus</u>

2. Timothy 1:16-18 WHAT did Onesiphorus do? <u>He was not ashamed. He refreshed Paul. He searched for him in Rome.</u>

WHO were the faithful and the unfaithful? Faithful: <u>Onesiphorus</u> Unfaithful: <u>All those in Asia, Phygelus and Hermogenes</u>

2 Timothy 1:17 WHERE was Onesiphorus when he found Paul? <u>In Rome</u>

WHERE is Paul in prison? <u>In Rome</u>

Don't forget to practice your memory verse.

(page 16)

2 Timothy 1:15 WHO are the people mentioned in this verse?

Guard the Treasure   17

1. All who are in <u>Asia</u>

2. P <u>h y g e l u s</u>

3. H <u>e r m o g e n e s</u>

2 Timothy 1:15 WHAT did this group of people in Asia do?

They <u>turned</u> <u>away</u> from Paul.

2 Timothy 1:16-18 WHO is the person mentioned in these verses?

<u>Onesiphorus</u>

2 Timothy 1:16-18 WHAT did Onesiphorus do? <u>He was not ashamed. He refreshed Paul. He searched for him in Rome.</u>

Did you see the contrast, the difference in these people? Those who were unfaithful turned away from Paul, but the one who was faithful was not ashamed of Paul. WHO was faithful? WHO supported Paul? And WHO are the unfaithful, those who turned away?

Faithful: <u>Onesiphorus</u>

Unfaithful: <u>All those in Asia, Phygelus and Hermogenes</u>

Now look at 2 Timothy 1:17. WHERE was Onesiphorus when he found Paul? <u>In Rome</u>

All right! You just uncovered another clue in our setting. You discovered WHERE Paul is.

WHERE is Paul in prison? <u>In Rome</u>

18   WEEK ONE

Way to go! Tomorrow we will continue to get the big picture of 2 Timothy. Don't forget to practice your memory verse!

(page 18)

DAY THREE
HIT THE TRAINING FIELD

12

"Hey, Max, that was an awesome long jump!" Molly told Max as they walked off the training field.

"Thanks, Molly. I noticed you cut a few seconds off your time as you were practicing your sprints," Max smiled.

"I can't believe it!" Molly handed Max a towel. "I guess all those exercises Coach Neighbors is making us do are paying off."

"They sure are. Coach Neighbors is not only a great teacher, teaching us the skills we need to improve in each one of our events. He's also a great encourager, just like Paul. We better get

WOW! GREAT TIME!

USA

to the showers and clean up so we can read more of Paul's letter to Timothy."

"All right. I'll meet you at Hardaway Hall."

Now that we have practiced for our events, let's get back to 2 Timothy. Training our minds and winning the gold for God takes hard work and self-discipline, just like training our bodies. Don't forget to talk to God and ask for His help.

We are ready to read another section of our letter. Turn to page 161 and read 2 Timothy 2. Mark Paul by coloring him blue, mark Timothy by coloring him orange, and color all the other people pink. Don't mark the soldier, athlete, and farmer pink— they aren't real people in the text; they are just illustrations. Don't forget to mark your pronouns!

Guided Instruction

DAY THREE

God sees and is pleased that you want to get to know Him better. Ask Him to give you a special message today.

12 Turn to page 18 and read "Hit the Training Field."

Guided Instruction

Turn to page 161 and read 2 Timothy 2 aloud using your Observation Worksheet visual aid as students follow along and call out each key word. Then mark them together as we noted on p. 13.

(page 161)

Chapter 2

1 You therefore, my son, be strong in the grace that is in Christ Jesus.

2 The things which you have heard from me in the presence of many witnesses, entrust these to faithful men who will be able to teach others also.

3 Suffer hardship with me, as a good soldier of Christ Jesus.

4 No soldier in active service entangles himself in the affairs of everyday life, so that he may please the one who enlisted him as a soldier.

5 Also if anyone competes as an athlete, he does not win the prize unless he competes according to the rules.

6 The hard-working farmer ought to be the first to receive his share of the crops.

162   *Observation Worksheets*

7 Consider what I say, for the Lord will give you understanding in everything.

8 Remember Jesus Christ, risen from the dead, descendant of David, according to my gospel,

9 for which I suffer hardship even to imprisonment as a criminal; but the word of God is not imprisoned.

10 For this reason I endure all things for the sake of those who are chosen, so that they also may obtain the salvation which is in Christ Jesus and with it eternal glory.

11 It is a trustworthy statement:
For if we died with Him, we will also live with Him;

12 If we endure, we will also reign with Him;
If we deny Him, He also will deny us;

13 If we are faithless, He remains faithful, for He cannot deny Himself.

14 Remind them of these things, and solemnly charge them in the presence of God not to wrangle about words, which is useless and leads to the ruin of the hearers.

15 Be diligent to present yourself approved to God as a workman who does not need to be ashamed, accurately handling the word of truth.

16 But avoid worldly and empty chatter, for it will lead to further ungodliness,

17 and their talk will spread like gangrene. Among them are Hymenaeus and Philetus,

18 men who have gone astray from the truth saying that the resurrection has already taken place, and they upset the faith of some.

(page 162)

Guided Instruction

rection has already taken place, and they upset the faith of some.

19 Nevertheless, the firm foundation of God stands, having this seal, "The Lord knows those who are His," and, "Everyone who names the name of the Lord is to abstain from wickedness."

20 Now in a large house there are not only gold and silver vessels,

Observation Worksheets—2 Timothy 163

but also vessels of wood and of earthenware, and some to honor and some to dishonor.

21 Therefore, if anyone cleanses himself from these things, he will be a vessel for honor, sanctified, useful to the Master, prepared for every good work.

22 Now flee from youthful lusts and pursue righteousness, faith, love and peace, with those who call on the Lord from a pure heart.

23 But refuse foolish and ignorant speculations, knowing that they produce quarrels.

24 The Lord's bond-servant must not be quarrelsome, but be kind to all, able to teach, patient when wronged,

25 with gentleness correcting those who are in opposition, if perhaps God may grant them repentance leading to the knowledge of the truth,

26 and they may come to their senses and escape from the snare of the devil, having been held captive by him to do his will.

Guided Instruction

14 Make a list in the box on page 19.

WHAT I Learned About Paul

2 Timothy 2:3 Paul <u>suffered</u> hardship as a good <u>soldier</u> of <u>Christ</u> <u>Jesus</u>.

2. Timothy 2:8-9 Paul <u>suffered</u> hardship even to <u>imprisonment</u> as a <u>criminal</u> for the g <u>o s p e l</u>.

2 Timothy 2:10 Paul <u>endured</u> all things for the sake of those who are <u>chosen</u>.

2 Timothy 2:1 HOW is Timothy described in this verse? He is Paul's <u>son</u>.

Read the selected verses to answer the questions.

Acts 16:1 A <u>disciple...</u>, the son of a <u>Jewish</u> woman who was a <u>believer</u>, but his father was a <u>Greek</u>.

Acts 16:2 Timothy was <u>well</u> <u>spoken</u> of by the <u>brothers</u>.

Acts 16:3 Paul c <u>i r c u m c i s e d</u> Timothy.

1 Corinthians 4:17 HOW is Timothy described? <u>Beloved and faithful child in the Lord</u>

(page 19)

…get to mark your pronouns.
Let's make a list on Paul in the box below.

14

> **WHAT I Learned About Paul**
>
> 2 Timothy 2:3 Paul ____**suffered**____ hardship as a good ____**soldier**____ of ____**Christ**____ ____**Jesus**____ .
>
> 2 Timothy 2:8-9 Paul ____**suffered**____ hardship even to ____**imprisonment**____ as a ____**criminal**____ for the g <u>o s p e l</u>.
>
> 2 Timothy 2:10 Paul ____**endured**____ all things for the sake of those who are ____**chosen**____ .

Only one thing is mentioned about Timothy in 2 Timothy 2. 2 Timothy 2:1 HOW is Timothy described in this verse?

He is Paul's **son**____.

The other places where we marked *Timothy* in 2 Timothy 2 contain instructions to Timothy rather than information about Timothy. So let's do some *cross-referencing* to get more information

---

20   WEEK ONE

about Timothy. Cross-referencing means looking at other passages of Scripture and comparing Scripture with Scripture.

Pull out your official Rulebook, your Bible. Look up and read Acts 16:1-5. HOW is Timothy described?

Acts 16:1 A ____**disciple...**____ , the son of a ____**Jewish**____ woman who was a ____**believer**____ , but his father was a ____**Greek**____ .

Acts 16:2 Timothy was ____**well**____ ____**spoken**____ of by the ____**brothers**____ .

Acts 16:3 Paul c <u>i r c u m c i s e d</u> Timothy.

Look up and read 1 Corinthians 4:17. HOW is Timothy described?

<u>Beloved and faithful child in the Lord</u>

_____

(page 20)

Look up and read Philippians 2:19-24.

WHAT do you learn about Timothy?

Philippians 2:20 Timothy is a _____**kindred**_____ ____**spirit**____ who will genuinely be ___**concerned**___ for other's____**welfare**____.

Philippians 2:22 Timothy has proven ____**worth**____. He s **e r v e** d with Paul in the _____**furtherance**_____ of the _____**gospel**_____ like a ____**child**____ serving his ____**father**____.

Amazing! Timothy is spoken well of, he has proven worth, and he genuinely cares for the welfare of others. Timothy has

---

Guard the Treasure 21

been faithful in serving with Paul in furthering the gospel. Are you like Timothy? Do you genuinely care for others? Name one way you care for other people. _____

_____

Now look at where you marked the other names in 2 Timothy 2.

2 Timothy 2:17-18 WHO are the people mentioned? **Ungodly men who have gone astray**

_____

2 Timothy 2:17-18 WHAT do we learn about these men? **Their talk will spread like gangrene. Two of them are Hymenaeus and Philetus. They have gone astray from the truth, upsetting the faith of some.** Are they teaching what is true? **No**

WHAT are they teaching that is untrue? **That the resurrection has already taken place**

_____

Do these men sound like "faithful men," true believers in Jesus? **No**

Guided Instruction

Philippians 2:19-24 WHAT do you learn about Timothy? Philippians 2:20 Timothy is a <u>kindred</u> <u>spirit</u> who will genuinely be <u>concerned</u> for other's <u>welfare</u>.

Philippians 2:22 Timothy has proven <u>worth</u>. He s <u>e r v e</u> d with Paul in the <u>furtherance</u> of the <u>gospel</u> like a <u>child</u> serving his <u>father</u>.

Lead a discussion about the next questions and have students respond independently.

Read the selected verses in Timothy to answer the questions on pages 21-22.

2 Timothy 2:17-18 WHO are the people mentioned? <u>Ungodly men who have gone astray</u>

2 Timothy 2:17-18 WHAT do we learn about these men? <u>Their talk will spread like gangrene. Two of them are Hymenaeus and Philetus. They have gone astray from the truth, upsetting the faith of some.</u>

Are they teaching what is true? <u>No</u>

WHAT are they teaching that is untrue? <u>That the resurrection has already taken place</u>

Do these men sound like faithful men, true believers in Jesus? <u>No</u>

Guided Instruction

WHAT word is repeated in 2 Timothy 1–2 and seems to be a very important subject in this letter? Paul is suffering for the g o s p e l.

What is the word on page 22?

T r e a s u r e

Practice saying the memory verse with a friend.

(page 21)

Great work! You got a few more pieces to Paul's letter. Have you noticed a word that is repeated in 2 Timothy 1–2 and that seems to be a very important subject in this letter? Fill in the blanks below if you know what this key word is.

Paul is suffering for the g o s p e l.

Now, keep your eyes open—you want to see if this word or

22   WEEK ONE

any synonyms for this word show up in the next two chapters of Paul's letter. By the way, one of the words in your memory verse is a synonym for this word. Do you know what the word is? Fill in the blanks if you do.

T r e a s u r e

Fantastic! Now go out and take a couple of laps around the track as you practice your memory verse!

DAY FOUR

15 ## PERSEVERE—DON'T GIVE UP!

"Okay, guys," Coach Neighbors called out. "You've done a great job on your relay drills today. Remember, when you get tired, hang in there—don't give up! Winning the race is about persevering even when you're tired and the going gets tough.

"Let's take a break, eat a snack, and give our bodies a little rest while we work on our letter of 2 Timothy. Then we'll head back for our afternoon training session."

All right! You are looking good out on the training field. Way to hang in there! Let's pray.

Now turn to page 163 and read 2 Timothy 3. Mark Paul by coloring him blue, color Timothy orange, and color all the other people pink. Don't forget to mark your pronouns!

Let's make a list on Paul.

(page 163)

16 **Chapter 3**

1 But realize this, that in the last days difficult times will come.

2 For men will be lovers of self, lovers of money, boastful, arrogant, revilers, disobedient to parents, ungrateful, unholy,

3 unloving, irreconcilable, malicious gossips, without self-control, brutal, haters of good,

4 treacherous, reckless, conceited, lovers of pleasure rather than lovers of God,

5 holding to a form of godliness, although they have denied its power; avoid such men as these.

6 For among them are those who enter into households and captivate weak women weighed down with sins, led on by various impulses,

Guided Instruction

DAY FOUR

Ask God to clear your mind and help you understand His Word.

15 Turn to page 23 and read "Persevere-Don't Give Up!"

16 Turn to page 163 and read 2 Timothy 3 aloud using your Observation Worksheet visual aid as students follow along and call out each key word. Then mark them together as we noted on p. 13.

Guided Instruction

17 Read the selected verses to make a list about Paul in the box.

WHAT I Learned About Paul

2 Timothy 3:11 Paul was <u>persecuted</u> and <u>suffered</u> at <u>Antioch</u>, <u>Iconium</u>, and at <u>Lystra</u>. Paul e <u>n</u> <u>d</u> <u>u</u> <u>r</u> <u>e</u> <u>d</u> his persecutions, and the L <u>o</u> <u>r</u> <u>d</u> <u>rescued</u> him.

---

164   *Observation Worksheets*

7 always learning and never able to come to the knowledge of the truth.

8 Just as Jannes and Jambres opposed Moses, so these men also oppose the truth, men of depraved mind, rejected in regard to the faith.

9 But they will not make further progress; for their folly will be obvious to all, just as Jannes's and Jambres's folly was also.

10 Now you followed my teaching, conduct, purpose, faith, patience, love, perseverance,

11 persecutions, and sufferings, such as happened to me at Antioch, at Iconium and at Lystra; what persecutions I endured, and out of them all the Lord rescued me!

12 Indeed, all who desire to live godly in Christ Jesus will be persecuted.

13 But evil men and impostors will proceed from bad to worse, deceiving and being deceived.

14 You, however, continue in the things you have learned and become convinced of, knowing from whom you have learned them,

15 and that from childhood you have known the sacred writings which are able to give you the wisdom that leads to salvation through faith which is in Christ Jesus.

16 All Scripture is inspired by God and profitable for teaching, for reproof, for correction, for training in righteousness;

17 so that the man of God may be adequate, equipped for every good work.

(page 23)

Let's make a list on Paul.

17 **WHAT I Learned About Paul**

2 Timothy 3:11 Paul was ____**persecuted**____ and ____**suffered**____ at ___**Antioch**___, ___**Iconium**___, and at ___**Lystra**___. Paul e **n** **d** **u** **r** **e** **d** his persecutions, and the L **o** **r** **d** ____**rescued**____ him.

WEEK ONE

24

Wow! Don't you want to be like Paul—able to endure all those persecutions and sufferings? Isn't it awesome to see that God rescued Paul out of all those persecutions!

Let's make a list on Timothy.

> ### WHAT I Learned About Timothy
>
> 2 Timothy 3:10-11 Timothy followed Paul's
>
> __teaching__ , __conduct__ , __purpose__ ,
> __faith__ , __patience__ , __love__ ,
> __perseverance__ , __persecutions__ and __sufferings__ .
>
> 2 Timothy 3:15 From c __h i l d h o o d__ Timothy
> has known the __sacred__ __writings__ .

Did you know that right now you are becoming a "Timothy"? Timothy learned God's Word in childhood. That's what you are doing right now!

And just WHO are the other people in 2 Timothy 3? HOW are they described?

2 Timothy 3:2 Men who are __lovers__ of __self__ , lovers of __money__ , __boastful__ , __arrogant__ , __revilers__ , __disobedient__ to parents, __ungrateful__ , __unholy__ ,

2 Timothy 3:3 __unloving__ , __irreconcilable__ , __malicious__ gossips, without __self__-__control__ , __brutal__ , __haters__ of __good__ ,

2 Timothy 3:4 __treacherous__ , __reckless__ ,

__conceited__ , lovers of __pleasure__ rather than lovers of __God__ ;

Guided Instruction

18 Read the selected verses to make a list about Timothy.

WHAT I Learned About Timothy

2 Timothy 3:10-11 Timothy followed Paul's <u>teaching</u>, <u>conduct</u>, <u>purpose</u>, <u>faith</u>, <u>patience</u>, <u>love</u>, <u>perseverance</u>. <u>persecutions</u>, and <u>sufferings</u>.

2 Timothy 3:15 From c h i l d h o o d Timothy has known the <u>sacred</u> <u>writings</u>.

WHO are other people in 2 Timothy 3? HOW are they described?

2 Timothy 3:2 Men who are <u>lovers</u> of <u>self</u>, lovers of <u>money</u>, <u>boastful</u>, <u>arrogant</u>, <u>revilers</u>, <u>disobedient</u> to parents, <u>ungrateful</u>, <u>unholy</u>

2 Timothy 3:3 <u>unloving</u>, <u>irreconcilable</u>, <u>malicious</u> gossips, without <u>self-control</u>, <u>brutal</u>, <u>haters</u> of <u>good</u>,

2 Timothy 3:4 <u>treacherous</u>, <u>reckless</u>, <u>conceited</u>, lovers of <u>pleasure</u> rather than lovers of <u>God</u>;

Guided Instruction

2 Timothy 3:5 holding to a form of <u>godliness</u> although they have <u>denied</u> its <u>power</u>.

2 Timothy 3:6 They enter households and <u>captivate</u> weak <u>women</u>.

2 Timothy 3:7 They are always <u>learning</u> and never able to come to the <u>knowledge</u> of the <u>truth</u>.

2 Timothy 3:8 They are like <u>Jannes</u> and <u>Jambres</u>, who opposed Moses. These men <u>oppose</u> the <u>truth</u>, men of <u>depraved</u> <u>minds</u>, rejected in regard to the <u>faith</u>.

2 Timothy 3:9 They will not make further <u>progress</u>; for their <u>folly</u> will be <u>obvious</u> to all.

2 Timothy 3:13 <u>Evil</u> men and <u>imposters</u> will proceed from <u>bad</u> to <u>worse</u>, <u>deceiving</u> and being <u>deceived</u>.

2 Timothy 3:5 WHAT does Paul tell Timothy to do? <u>Avoid such men as these</u>

WHO are these men? <u>Unbelievers</u>

(page 25)

2 Timothy 3:5 holding to a form of ___godliness___, although they have ___denied___ its ___power___.

2 Timothy 3:6 They enter households and ___captivate___ weak ___women___.

2 Timothy 3:7 They are always ___learning___ and never able to come to the ___knowledge___ of the ___truth___.

2 Timothy 3:8 They are like ___Jannes___ and ___Jambres___, who opposed Moses. These men ___oppose___ the ___truth___, men of ___depraved___ ___minds___, rejected in regard to the ___faith___.

2 Timothy 3:9 They will not make further ___progress___; for their ___folly___ will be ___obvious___ to all.

2 Timothy 3:13 ___Evil___ men and ___imposters___ will proceed from ___bad___ to ___worse___, ___deceiving___ and being ___deceived___.

2 Timothy 3:5 WHAT does Paul tell Timothy to do? ___Avoid such men as these___

26   WEEK ONE

Now, from the way these men are described, WHO are these men—believers in Jesus or unbelievers?

___Unbelievers___

Whew! Are you beginning to see WHY Paul is writing to Timothy? Think about what Paul keeps talking about, and think about these people you have been marking. If you don't see it right now, you will as you keep on studying. We are so proud of you! Keep up the good work. Tomorrow we will read the rest of Paul's letter to Timothy.

Now head back to the training field. Coach Neighbors is waiting to see just how many ankle jumps you can do while you say your verse.

(page 26)

Guided Instruction

DAY FIVE

19 **GET READY TO RUN!**

"Okay, team, today is our last day of practice. Tonight is the opening ceremony for our summer games, and then it will be time for the games to begin. Are you ready?"

"We're ready, Coach!" all the kids yelled out while Sam started jumping up and down, barking, and turning in circles.

Coach Neighbors laughed. "Looks like Sam is more than ready. Let's line up with our teams and rehearse tonight's opening."

"Great rehearsal! Max, why don't you lead everyone back inside and pray so we can wrap up our overview—the big picture on Paul's letter. Next week as we begin our games, we will start looking at the details."

"Yes, sir!" Max answered. "All right, let's head back to Hardaway Hall. Last one there has to give Sam a bath."

Guard the Treasure 27

Immediately everyone started running. No one wants to bathe Sam—you know how he hates baths!

You made it! Thank heaven you ran so fast—now you won't have to bathe Sam. Today we are going to finish reading Paul's letter to get the big picture of WHY Paul wrote this letter to Timothy. Don't forget to ask God for His help.

Then turn to page 164 and read 2 Timothy 4. Mark Paul by coloring him blue, color Timothy orange, and color all the other people pink. Don't forget to mark your pronouns!

Let's make a list on Paul in the box below.

DAY FIVE

What a study! You can see how ungodly men deny the truth of God's Word. Ask God to keep you in His care and protect you from such lies.

19 Turn to page 26 and read "Get Ready to Run."

Guided Instruction

 Turn to page 164 and read 2 Timothy 4 aloud using your Observation Worksheet visual aid as students follow along and call out each key word. Then mark them together as we noted on p. 13.

Paul (color blue)

Timothy (color orange)

all the other people (color pink)

(page 164)

20

Chapter 4

1 I solemnly charge you in the presence of God and of Christ Jesus, who is to judge the living and the dead, and by His appearing and His kingdom:

Observation Worksheets—2 Timothy   165

2 preach the word; be ready in season and out of season; reprove, rebuke, exhort, with great patience and instruction.

3 For the time will come when they will not endure sound doctrine; but wanting to have their ears tickled, they will accumulate for themselves teachers in accordance to their own desires,

4 and will turn away their ears from the truth and will turn aside to myths.

5 But you, be sober in all things, endure hardship, do the work of an evangelist, fulfill your ministry.

6 For I am already being poured out as a drink offering, and the time of my departure has come.

7 I have fought the good fight, I have finished the course, I have kept the faith;

8 in the future there is laid up for me the crown of righteousness, which the Lord, the righteous Judge, will award to me on that day; and not only to me, but also to all who have loved His appearing.

9 Make every effort to come to me soon;

10 for Demas, having loved this present world, has deserted me and gone to Thessalonica; Crescens has gone to Galatia, Titus to Dalmatia.

11 Only Luke is with me. Pick up Mark and bring him with you, for he is useful to me for service.

12 But Tychicus I have sent to Ephesus.

13 When you come bring the cloak which I left at Troas with Carpus, and the books, especially the parchments.

14 Alexander the coppersmith did me much harm; the Lord will repay him according to his deeds.

15 Be on guard against him yourself, for he vigorously opposed our teaching.

16 At my first defense no one supported me, but all deserted me; may it not be counted against them.

166   *Observation Worksheets*

17 But the Lord stood with me and strengthened me, so that through me the proclamation might be fully accomplished, and that all the Gentiles might hear; and I was rescued out of the lion's mouth.

18 The Lord will rescue me from every evil deed, and will bring me safely to His heavenly kingdom; to Him be the glory forever and ever. Amen.

19 Greet Prisca and Aquila, and the household of Onesiphorus.

20 Erastus remained at Corinth, but Trophimus I left sick at Miletus.

21 Make every effort to come before winter. Eubulus greets you, also Pudens and Linus and Claudia and all the brethren.

22 The Lord be with your spirit. Grace be with you.

(page 27)

people pink. Don't forget to mark your pronouns!
Let's make a list on Paul in the box below.

21   **WHAT I Learned About Paul**

2 Timothy 4:1 Paul ___charged___ Timothy in the presence of ___God___ and ___Christ___ ___Jesus___.

2 Timothy 4:6 Paul is being ___poured___ out as a ___drink___ ___offering___. It is the time of Paul's ___departure___.

2 Timothy 4:7 Paul has ___fought___ the ___good___ ___fight___, he has ___finished___ the ___course___, he has kept the ___faith___.

2 Timothy 4:8 In the future, Paul will receive the ___crown___ of ___righteousness___.

2 Timothy 4:10 Paul has been d e s e r t e d.

2 Timothy 4:11 Only ___Luke___ is with Paul. He wants Timothy to pick up and bring ___Mark___ with him.

2 Timothy 4:12 Paul sent ___Tychicus___ to ___Ephesus___.

Guided Instruction

21 Complete the list about Paul on page 27.

WHAT I Learned About Paul

2 Timothy 4:1 Paul <u>charged</u> Timothy in the presence of <u>God</u> and <u>Christ</u> <u>Jesus</u>.

2 Timothy 4:6 Paul is being <u>poured</u> out as a <u>drink</u> <u>offering</u>. It is the time of Paul's <u>departure</u>.

2 Timothy 4:7 Paul has <u>fought</u> the <u>good</u> <u>fight</u>, he has <u>finished</u> the <u>course</u>, he has kept the <u>faith</u>.

2 Timothy 4:8 In the future, Paul will receive the <u>crown</u> of <u>righteousness</u>.

2 Timothy 4:8 Paul has been d <u>e</u> <u>s</u> <u>e</u> <u>r</u> <u>t</u> <u>e</u> <u>d</u>.

2 Timothy 4:11 Only <u>Luke</u> is with Paul. He wants Timothy to pick up and bring <u>Mark</u> with him.

2 Timothy 4:12 Paul sent <u>Tychicus</u> to <u>Ephesus</u>.

Guided Instruction

2 Timothy 4:13 Paul left his <u>cloak</u> at Troas with Carpus. He wants Timothy to bring his c <u>l o a k</u>, his <u>books</u>, and especially the <u>parchments</u>.

2 Timothy 4:14 <u>Alexander</u> the coppersmith did Paul <u>much</u> <u>harm</u>.

2 Timothy 4:16 No one <u>supported</u> Paul; all <u>deserted</u> him.

2 Timothy 4:17 The <u>Lord</u> stood with Paul and <u>strengthened</u> Paul. Paul was <u>rescued</u> out of the <u>lion's</u> mouth.

WHAT do we see about the other people in 2 Timothy 4:3-4? The time will come when they will not <u>endure</u> <u>sound</u> <u>doctrine</u>. They will want to have their <u>ears</u> <u>tickled</u>. They will accumulate <u>teachers</u> in accordance with their own <u>desires</u> and will <u>turn</u> <u>away</u> their <u>ears</u> from the <u>truth</u> and will turn aside to <u>myths</u>.

2 Timothy 4:10 WHAT did Demas do?
<u>Deserted Paul</u>

---

28 _____ WEEK ONE _____

2 Timothy 4:13 Paul left his ____**cloak**____ at Troas with Carpus. He wants Timothy to bring his c _l o a k_, his ____**books**____, and especially the ____**parchments**____.

2 Timothy 2:14 ____**Alexander**____ the coppersmith did Paul ____**much**____ ____**harm**____.

2 Timothy 4:16 No one ____**supported**____ Paul; all ____**deserted**____ him.

2 Timothy 4:17 The ____**Lord**____ stood with Paul and ____**strengthened**____ Paul. Paul was ____**rescued**____ out of the ____**lion's**____ mouth.

Amazing! Paul's time to die has come, but he has been faithful to God. He has fought the good fight and finished the course even though he has suffered and been deserted by other people. Paul has gone for the gold! What about you? Don't you want to go for the gold too?

WHAT do we see about the other people in 2 Timothy 4:3-4?

The time will come when they will not ____**endure**____ ____**sound**____ ____**doctrine**____. They will want to have their ____**ears**____ ____**tickled**____. They will accumulate ____**teachers**____ in accordance with their own ____**desires**____ and will ____**turn**____ ____**away**____ their ____**ears**____ from the ____**truth**____ and will turn aside to ____**myths**____.

2 Timothy 4:10 WHAT did Demas do?

_____**Deserted Paul**_____

2 Timothy 4:14-15 WHAT about Alexander the copper-smith? WHAT did he do? **Opposed Paul's teaching. He did Paul harm.**

Whoa, these men don't want to hear the truth! Instead, they turn aside from truth to myths. Demas loved the world, and Alexander did Paul harm. Have you noticed as we have read this letter that there are a lot of unfaithful people in the church and only a very few faithful ones? WHY do you think some stay faithful while others turn away? Could knowing God's Word, the truth, make a difference?

WHAT do you think? _____

_____

Now that we have read all of 2 Timothy, let's review what we have learned this week as we saw the big picture. Let's review by asking the 5 W's and an H questions.

WHO wrote the letter? **Paul**

To WHOM was the letter written? **Timothy**

WHERE is Paul? **In Rome**

HOW is Paul being treated? **He is suffering hardship**

Look at 2 Timothy 1:8 and 2 Timothy 2:8-10. WHY is Paul in prison?
For the Gospel

2 Timothy 4:6 WHEN is this happening?

Paul says, "The time of my **departure** has come."

Guided Instruction

2 Timothy 4:14-15 WHAT about Alexander the coppersmith? WHAT did he do? Opposed Paul's teaching. He did Paul harm.

Discuss the next question with students. Have them respond independently.

Review the big picture of 2 Timothy.

WHO wrote the letter? Paul

To WHOM was the letter written? Timothy

WHERE is Paul? In Rome

HOW is Paul being treated? He is suffering hardship

2 Timothy 1:8 and 2 Timothy 2:8-10 WHY is Paul in prison? For the Gospel

2 Timothy 4:6 WHEN is this happening? Paul says, "The time of my departure has come."

Guided Instruction

22 Read the information about Nero on page 30.

WHAT is the historical setting? WHAT is happening to Paul? <u>Christians were being persecuted</u>.

Some were f <u>a</u> <u>i</u> <u>t</u> <u>h</u> <u>f</u> <u>u</u> <u>l</u> men, and some were u <u>n</u> <u>f</u> <u>a</u> <u>i</u> <u>t</u> <u>h</u> <u>f</u> <u>u</u> <u>l</u> men who turned away and opposed the truth.

2 Timothy 3:5 WHAT did Paul tell Timothy to do? A <u>v</u> <u>o</u> <u>i</u> <u>d</u> such <u>men</u> as these

Take a look at Max and Molly's notes below to gain more insight on what was happening at this time in history.

22

Nero the Roman Emperor

Nero was the Roman emperor at this time in history. Nero set a large majority of the city of Rome on fire and blamed the Christians in order to keep people from being suspicious of what he had done. He ordered Christians to be imprisoned and executed. Many Christians were put on poles alongside the highway and then, while they were still alive, they were set on fire to become human torches!

WHAT is the historical setting of this letter? WHAT is happening to Paul? Is this a time of persecution? Write out WHAT is happening at this time in history.

<u>Christians were being persecuted.</u>

WHAT did we learn about the other people that Paul talked about in his letter? Some were f <u>a i t h f u l</u> men, and some were u <u>n f a i t h f u l</u> men who turned away and opposed the truth. Do you think Paul might be warning Timothy about these unfaithful men in the church, men who teach things that aren't true?

Look back at 2 Timothy 3:5. WHAT did Paul tell Timothy to do?

A <u>v o i d</u> such ____ **men** ____ as these.

WHAT is the main thing 2 Timothy is about? Think about what Paul has repeated in his letter. Think about your memory verse too.

WHAT is Paul telling Timothy to do? **Not be ashamed of the testimony of Jesus; guard the treasure entrusted to you, to suffer for the Gospel**

All right! You now have the big picture of Paul's letter to Timothy. You have discovered that Paul is writing to Timothy, his beloved son in the faith, because he is in prison, suffering for the gospel. Paul knows that he is about to die, so he is passing the baton on to Timothy. Do you know what it means to "pass the baton" on to someone? To pass the baton is to give the responsibility for something important to another person.

In a relay race, passing the baton is where one runner hands his baton to the next runner so the next runner can continue the race. Passing the baton is the most crucial part of the relay race. It is so important that track coaches spend hours training athletes how to transfer the baton from one runner to the next and continue the race at full speed. If the baton isn't passed inside the passing zone or it is dropped, the team will lose the race. The trick to winning the race is the passing of the baton.

Paul wants to help Timothy fulfill his responsibility to the

Guided Instruction

WHAT is the main thing 2 Timothy is about? WHAT is Paul telling Timothy to do? Not be ashamed of the testimony of Jesus; guard the treasure entrusted to you, to suffer for the Gospel

Read and discuss the rest of the text in this chapter.

If you are a classroom teacher you may want to give your students a quiz on their memory verse. There is also a quiz on Week One on page 155 to check memory and understanding.

If you are a Sunday School teacher this is a great time to review the whole week by playing a game like *The Matching Game* on page 164 or *M&M® Draw* on page 165. This is also a great way for classroom teachers and homeschool families to review with students what they learned this week

Memory Verse

"Guard through the Holy Spirit who dwells in us the treasure which has been entrusted to you."

2 Timothy 1:14

Guided Instruction

gospel. Paul is passing the baton to Timothy, telling him to guard the treasure that has been entrusted to him.

How about you? Are you willing to take the baton of the gospel and pass it on to others? Do you know what the treasure, the gospel, is? You'll find out as we look at all the details in 2 Timothy 1 next week.

Don't forget your training to become God's champion. Say your memory verse out loud to some grown-ups this week. Ask them how they are guarding the treasure that has been entrusted to them.

2

DON'T BE ASHAMED

23

2 TIMOTHY 1

Wow! Wasn't that an awesome opening ceremony with all those cool fireworks? You did a fantastic job running in with the torch! Weren't you proud of Sam, all shiny and clean, wearing his USA bandana and walking so respectfully beside Max as he carried in the flag for the United States? It was so much fun watching all the kids walk in, representing different countries of the world and bringing us all together as one!

33

Guided Instruction

WEEK 2

DAY ONE

What a privilege to study God's Holy Word. Ask him to give you focus and clear understanding.

23 Turn to page 33 and read "2 Timothy 1." Then read "The Games Begin!" on the next page.

Guided Instruction

Last week as we began reading Paul's letter to Timothy, we got the big picture. This week we are going to start filling in the details so we can learn how to guard the treasure and become champions for God. We have opened the games, so let the competition begin!

DAY ONE

THE GAMES BEGIN!

"Run, Molly, run!" Max, Matthew, and Molly's other teammates yelled out as Molly took off out of the starting blocks.

"She did it!" Matthew high-fived Max. "Our first race, and Molly came in first place. Our first gold medal! Way to go, Molly!"

Wasn't that exciting? Now it's time to get back to our training in 2 Timothy. Don't forget to pray and thank God for giving you a strong mind and a healthy body to serve Him. Then ask Him to help you to understand His Word.

Fantastic! Today we are going to mark key words. What are key words? Key words are words that pop up more than once. They help unlock the meaning of the chapter or book you are studying and give you clues about what is most important in a passage of Scripture.

- Key words are usually used over and over again. (That's because God doesn't want you to miss the point.)

- Key words are important.

- Key words are used by the writer for a reason.

When you discover a key word, you need to mark it in a special way using a special color or symbol so you can immediately spot it in Scripture.

You may also want to make a bookmark for these key words

Guided Instruction

24 Discuss the information about key words and synonyms on pages 34-35.

If you have a whiteboard in your classroom you may want to list the key words and how to mark them on the whiteboard. Or you can have your students or child make a key word bookmark for these key words so they can see them at a glance as they mark them on their Observation Worksheets. To make a key word bookmark, get an index card or a piece of paper and write the key words listed below as well as how they are going to mark them on their Observations Worksheets.

God (Father, Lord) draw a purple triangle and color it yellow

Christ Jesus (and any other words that refer to Jesus, like Lord) draw a purple cross and color it yellow

remember (and the synonyms: recall, mindful, remind) circle it blue

Don't forget to mark your pronouns! And mark anything that tells you WHEN by drawing a green clock or green circle.

---

so you can see them at a glance as you mark them on your Observation Worksheets.

To make a key-word bookmark, get an index card or a piece of paper and write the key words listed below. Mark them with the colors and symbols you are going to use on your Observation Worksheets.

When you mark your key words, you will also need to mark any other words that mean the same thing, like pronouns or synonyms. You learned what pronouns were last week when you marked Paul and Timothy. Take a look at Molly and Max's training manual below to learn about synonyms.

24

Synonyms

Synonyms are different words that mean the same thing. *Sailboat*, *yacht*, and *rowboat* are all different words, but they all refer to boats. They are synonyms—ways to say the same thing with different words.

Great! Now, turn to page 160. Read 2 Timothy 1:1-7 and mark the key words and synonyms we have listed for you below.

God (Father, Lord) (draw a purple triangle and color it yellow)

Christ Jesus (and any other words that refer to Jesus, like *Lord*) (draw a purple cross and color it yellow)

remember (and the synonyms: recall, mindful, remind) (circle it in blue)

Don't forget to mark your pronouns! And mark anything that tells you WHEN by drawing a green clock 🕐 or green circle like this: ○ .

All right! Now, let's mark the 5 W's and an H to solve the cross-

Guided Instruction

25 Turn to page 160 and read 2 Timothy 1:1-7 aloud using your Observation Worksheet visual aid as students follow along and call out each key word. Then mark them together as we noted on p. 13.

(page 160)

OBSERVATION WORKSHEETS
2 TİMOTHY

25 Chapter 1

1 Paul, an apostle of Christ Jesus by the will of God, according to the promise of life in Christ Jesus,

27 2 To Timothy, my beloved son: Grace, mercy and peace from God the Father and Christ Jesus our Lord.

3 I thank God, whom I serve with a clear conscience the way my forefathers did, as I constantly remember you in my prayers night and day,

4 longing to see you, even as I recall your tears, so that I may be filled with joy.

5 For I am mindful of the sincere faith within you, which first dwelt in your grandmother Lois and your mother Eunice, and I am sure that it is in you as well.

28 6 For this reason I remind you to kindle afresh the gift of God which is in you through the laying on of my hands.

7 For God has not given us a spirit of timidity, but of power and love and discipline.

8 Th...

(page 35)

All right! Now, let's ask the 5 W's and an H to solve the crossword puzzle below.

2 Timothy 1:2 HOW does Paul greet Timothy? WHAT does he say to Timothy, his beloved son?

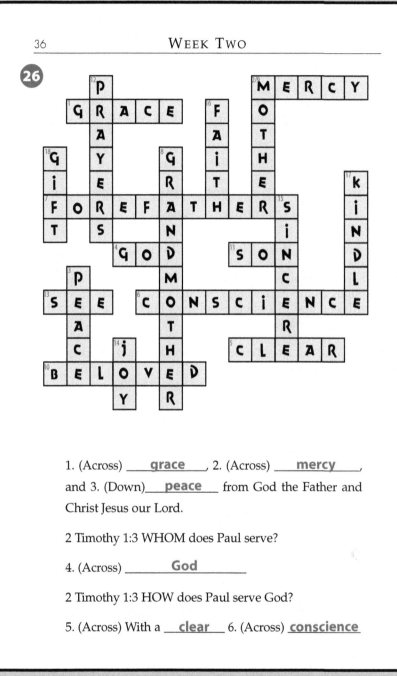

36   WEEK TWO

1. (Across) ____**grace**____, 2. (Across) ____**mercy**____, and 3. (Down)____**peace**____ from God the Father and Christ Jesus our Lord.

2 Timothy 1:3 WHOM does Paul serve?

4. (Across) _____**God**_____

2 Timothy 1:3 HOW does Paul serve God?

5. (Across) With a ___**clear**___ 6. (Across) **conscience**

Guided Instruction

26 Reread the selected verses to answer the questions and solve the crossword puzzle on page 36.

2 Timothy 1:2 HOW does Paul greet Timothy? WHAT does he say to Timothy?

1. (Across) grace, **2. (Across)** mercy, and **3. (Down)** peace from God the Father and Christ Jesus our Lord.

2 Timothy 1:3 WHOM does Paul serve?

4. (Across) God

2 Timothy 1:3 HOW does Paul serve God?

5. (Across) With a clear **6. (Across)** conscience

Guided Instruction

2 Timothy 1:3 WHERE does Paul get his example? WHOM does Paul compare himself with?

7. (Across) His f o r e f a t h e r s

2 Timothy 1:5 WHERE does Timothy get his example? WHERE did Timothy get his sincere faith?

8. (Down) His <u>grandmother</u> Lois, and his

9. (Down) <u>mother</u> Eunice.

2 Timothy 1:2 HOW does Paul encourage Timothy? WHAT does Paul call Timothy?

10. (Across) My <u>beloved</u> **11. (Across)** <u>son</u>

27 Draw a pink cloud around Timothy, my beloved son. (Teacher Guide page 44)

2 Timothy 1:3 HOW does Paul remember Timothy?

12. (Down) I constantly remember you in my <u>prayers</u> night and day.

Don't Be Ashamed   37

2 Timothy 1:3 WHERE does Paul get his example? WHOM does Paul compare himself with?

7. (Across) His f <u>o r e f a t h e r s</u>

2 Timothy 1:5 WHERE does Timothy get his example? WHERE did Timothy get his sincere faith?

8. (Down) His <u>grandmother</u> Lois, and his

9. (Down) <u>mother</u> Eunice.

Now, think about the things Paul is saying to Timothy. Do you know what Paul is doing? Paul is exhorting Timothy. An exhortation is an encouragement. An encouragement affirms us. It builds us up. An encouragement includes sincere and honest words of praise, like telling people how kind they are or that they are doing a great job.

Paul has a very important message for Timothy in his letter. But before Paul gives Timothy this message, Paul encourages and affirms Timothy.

Let's look at HOW Paul encourages Timothy.

Look at 2 Timothy 1:2 HOW does Paul encourage Timothy? WHAT does Paul call Timothy?

10. (Across) My <u>beloved</u> 11. (Across) <u>son</u>

Wow! Paul reminds Timothy of his love and Timothy's importance to him. Timothy is his beloved son. Isn't it *awesome* when people remind you they love you and that you are special to them?

Turn to your Observation Worksheet on page 160 and draw a pink cloud around this encouragement: *Timothy, my beloved son.*

2 Timothy 1:3 HOW does Paul remember Timothy?

I constantly remember you in my 12. (Down) <u>prayers</u> night and day.

Guided Instruction

38   WEEK TWO

2 Timothy 1:4 WHAT is Paul longing for?

13. (Across) To _____see_____ Timothy

2 Timothy 1:4 WHAT will seeing Timothy fill Paul with?

14. (Down) _____joy_____

Wouldn't it encourage you to know that someone close to you is praying for you, that they long to see you, and they are filled with joy when they see you?

Now draw a pink cloud around each one of these encouraging phrases on page 160.

2 Timothy 1:5 WHAT is Paul mindful of in Timothy?

15. (Down) His _____sincere_____ 16. (Down) _____faith_____

Paul tells Timothy that he knows Timothy's faith is real! Don't you want people to be able to see that you have a faith that is real?

Draw a pink cloud around these encouraging words on page 160.

2 Timothy 1:6 WHAT is Paul's encouragement in this verse? WHAT is Paul reminding Timothy to do?

17. (Down) To _____kindle_____ afresh the 18. (Down) _____gift_____ of God.

Paul is reminding Timothy to "kindle afresh" the gift of God. To "kindle afresh" means to stir up his gift like stirring up the embers of a fire to get the fire blazing.

WHAT is this gift Paul is talking about? We'll find out tomorrow! For now, draw a pink cloud around these encouraging words on page 160.

You have done an awesome job reading Paul's letter and discovering how Paul encouraged Timothy, showing him how

---

2 Timothy 1:4 WHAT is Paul longing for?

13. (Across) To <u>see</u> Timothy

2 Timothy 1:4 WHAT will seeing Timothy fill Paul with?

14. (Down) <u>joy</u>

2 Timothy 1:5 WHAT is Paul mindful of in Timothy?

15. (Down) His <u>sincere</u> **16. (Down)** <u>faith</u>

2 Timothy 1:6 WHAT is Paul's encouragement in this verse? WHAT is Paul reminding Timothy to do?

17. (Down) To <u>kindle</u> afresh the **18. (Down)** <u>gift</u> of God.

28 Draw a pink cloud around these encouraging words on page 160. (Teacher Guide page 44)

Guided Instruction

Read and discuss the rest of the text in this lesson.

much he loved and prayed for Timothy and reminding him of his faith and his gift.

How about you? Can you encourage someone today? Maybe you can encourage a kid at school who doesn't have a lot of confidence, or a friend who is having a hard time. Sometimes kids are mean to other kids and make fun of them. You could encourage others by saying something nice to them to show them that they are special and valuable to God. Or you could encourage your mom or dad by telling them that you love them and are thankful for them.

Think of some people you can encourage today. Tell them how good they are at sports or art or something else. Remind them that you like to hang out with them. Write a note to your parents and tell them what a good job they are doing, what they mean to you, and how thankful you are for them. Reach out and show God's love by making someone feel special today!

Way to go! Before you head off to our next event in our summer games, let's see if you can solve this week's memory verse.

Look at the track on the next page. Follow the letters around the track. Begin at the start position. Cross out every other letter. Go from the inside track, following the arrows. When you finish, put the letters that remain on the blanks below to spell out your verse. Then look up 2 Timothy 1 and find the reference for this verse.

40   WEEK TWO

29

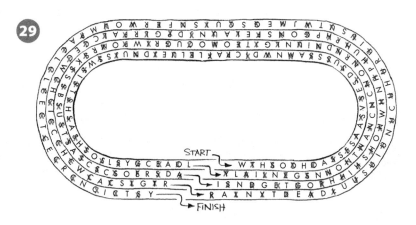

START

FINISH

30 w̲ h̲o̲ h̲a̲s̲ s̲a̲v̲e̲d̲ u̲s̲ a̲n̲d̲

c̲a̲l̲l̲e̲d̲ u̲s̲ w̲i̲t̲h̲ a̲ h̲o̲l̲y̲

c̲a̲l̲l̲i̲n̲g, n̲o̲t̲ a̲c̲c̲o̲r̲d̲i̲n̲g̲

t̲o̲ o̲u̲r̲ w̲o̲r̲k̲s, b̲u̲t̲

a̲c̲c̲o̲r̲d̲i̲n̲g̲ t̲o̲ H̲i̲s̲ o̲w̲n̲

p̲u̲r̲p̲o̲s̲e̲ a̲n̲d̲ g̲r̲a̲c̲e̲ w̲h̲i̲c̲h̲

w̲a̲s̲ g̲r̲a̲n̲t̲e̲d̲ u̲s̲ i̲n̲ C̲h̲r̲i̲s̲t̲

J̲e̲s̲u̲s̲ f̲r̲o̲m̲ a̲l̲l̲ e̲t̲e̲r̲n̲i̲t̲y̲

2 Timothy 1: _9_

Now write this verse out and practice saying it three times in a row out loud today!

Guided Instruction

29 Solve the memory verse on page 40.

W̲h̲o̲ h̲a̲s̲ s̲a̲v̲e̲d̲ u̲s̲ a̲n̲d̲ c̲a̲l̲l̲e̲d̲ u̲s̲ w̲i̲t̲h̲ a̲ h̲o̲l̲y̲ c̲a̲l̲l̲i̲n̲g̲, n̲o̲t̲ a̲c̲c̲o̲r̲d̲i̲n̲g̲ t̲o̲ o̲u̲r̲ w̲o̲r̲k̲s̲, b̲u̲t̲ a̲c̲c̲o̲r̲d̲i̲n̲g̲ t̲o̲ H̲i̲s̲ o̲w̲n̲ p̲u̲r̲p̲o̲s̲e̲ a̲n̲d̲ g̲r̲a̲c̲e̲ w̲h̲i̲c̲h̲ w̲a̲s̲ g̲r̲a̲n̲t̲e̲d̲ u̲s̲ i̲n̲ C̲h̲r̲i̲s̲t̲ J̲e̲s̲u̲s̲ f̲r̲o̲m̲ a̲l̲l̲ e̲t̲e̲r̲n̲i̲t̲y̲.

2 Timothy 1:9

30 Copy the memory verse to an index card and practice saying it three times, three times a day.

Guided Instruction

DAY TWO

Ask God to give you a personal message today.

31 Turn to page 41 and read "Stretch… Use That Gift for God."

Look up the selected cross-references and answer the questions.

1 Peter 4:10 WHAT does each one receive? A <u>special</u> <u>gift</u>

1 Peter 4:10 HOW are we to use that gift? To <u>serve</u> one another as <u>good</u> <u>stewards</u> of the manifold grace of God

1 Peter 4:11 WHY are we to use these gifts? So that in <u>all</u> <u>things</u> <u>God</u> may be <u>glorified</u> through <u>Jesus</u> <u>Christ</u>

Don't Be Ashamed   41

DAY TWO

31 STRETCH…USE THAT GIFT FOR GOD

Hey, guys! Wasn't it an awesome day in our track and field events? That was one incredible long jump as you stretched out in the air to land the gold medal! Sam just can't wait to congratulate you with a good face licking!

Let's celebrate while we continue our training in 2 Timothy 1 so we can win the gold for God. Yesterday, as we opened Paul's letter to Timothy, we saw how Paul loved and encouraged Timothy. He reminded Timothy to kindle afresh the gift of God.

Today we need to find out HOW Paul encouraged Timothy to use his gift. But first, is Timothy the only one who has a gift? Let's find out. Don't forget to talk to God!

Let's look at some cross-references. Pull out your official Rulebook, your Bible, and look up 1 Peter 4:10-11.

1 Peter 4:10 WHAT does each one receive?

A _____**special**_____ _____**gift**_____

1 Peter 4:10 HOW are we to use that gift?

To ____**serve**____ one another as ____**good**____ ____**stewards**____ of the manifold grace of God.

1 Peter 4:11 WHY are we to use these gifts?

So that in ____**all**____ ____**things**____ ____**God**____ may be ____**glorified**____ through ____**Jesus**____ ____**Christ**____.

Guided Instruction

2 Timothy 1:7 WHAT has God not given us? A spirit of timidity

Psalm 56:3 WHAT does this verse tell us to do when we are afraid? Put our trust in God

2 Timothy 1:7 WHAT has God given us? A spirit of power and love and discipline

Acts 1:8 HOW do we receive this power? WHERE do we get our power from? The Holy Spirit

---

42   WEEK TWO

Isn't that exciting? Timothy isn't the only one who gets a gift. God gives each one of us a gift when we accept Jesus Christ as our Savior.

But this gift isn't meant to make us feel good about ourselves. We are to use our gifts to serve one another and to bring God glory. Paul is encouraging Timothy to use the gift God has given Him.

HOW does Paul encourage Timothy to use this special gift? Turn to page 160 and read 2 Timothy 1:6-7. WHAT does Paul say to Timothy?

2 Timothy 1:7 WHAT has God *not* given us?

A __spirit__ of __timidity__

That means we are not to be afraid. God has not given us a spirit of fear. We are not to fear man or what man can do to us.

HOW can keep from being afraid? Look up and read Psalm 56:3-4.

Psalm 56:3 WHAT does this verse tell us to do when we are afraid?

__Put our trust in God__

Turn back to 2 Timothy 1:7 on page 160.
WHAT has God given us?

A spirit of __power__ and __love__ and __discipline__

So HOW do we have power? Look up and read Acts 1:8.

HOW do we receive power? WHERE do we get our power from? __The Holy Spirit__

Guided Instruction

WHAT does he give us? P o w e r

WHAT are we to be? Jesus' witnesses

2 Timothy 1:7 WHAT else do we have besides power? L o v e

1 John 4:10-11 WHAT did God do to show His love for us? He sent His Son for the propitiation of our sins.

Don't Be Ashamed   43

Amazing! When we accept Jesus Christ as our Savior, the Holy Spirit comes and lives in us (John 14:23). And WHAT does He give us according to Acts 1:8?

P o w e r !

Acts 1:8 WHAT are we to be? Jesus' ___witnesses___

Because we have power through the Holy Spirit, we can be witnesses about WHO Jesus is and WHAT He did for us. God gives us His power so we can share the good news about Jesus with other people.

WHAT else does 2 Timothy 1:7 tell us we have besides power?

L o v e.

Look up and read 1 John 4:10-11.

WHAT did God do to show His love for us?

He sent His Son for the propitiation of our sins.

What does the word *propitiation* mean? That's a big word, isn't it? When you think of propitiation, think of someone being satisfied, someone being appeased, someone else making amends for a wrong.

Another word for propitiation is *atonement*. Atonement is a covering for sin. In the Old Testament, people offered animal sacrifices to make an atonement to cover sin until the perfect sacrifice, Jesus Christ, came to earth as a baby to grow up, live a sinless life, and die on a cross to take away the sins of the whole world forever.

Sin separates us from God, but because God loves us, He gave His only Son, Jesus, to die on a cross and be the propitiation (atonement) for our sins. His blood doesn't just cover our sins; it takes them away forever and makes us right with God!

44   WEEK TWO

1 John 4:11 WHAT are we to do since God loves us?

Love one another

Read 1 John 4:18. WHAT do we see about love in this verse?

There is no fear in love. Perfect love casts out fear.

Because of God's great love and sacrifice for us, we do not have to be afraid. Perfect love casts out fear. And because of God's great love for us, we are to love others!

Now let's look at 2 Timothy 1:7 again and find the last thing Paul tells Timothy God has given us. WHAT else has God given us?

D i s c i p l i n e.

WHAT does this word mean? It means to have a sound mind, to have self-control. It describes people who have their mind under control. For example, suppose your mom makes you angry, and you want to yell at her or slam the door to your room. But instead of yelling or slamming your door, you decide to talk to her in a respectful way. That's what it means to have your mind under control. You want to say or do something hurtful, but you don't. Think about it. An athlete has to train his mind. HOW can we be disciplined? How can we have a steadfast mind?

Look up and read Isaiah 26:3.

HOW do we have a steadfast mind?

By trusting in God

Fantastic! You have seen Paul encourage Timothy to use his gift by showing Timothy he has everything he needs. Timothy has God's power, he has love, and he has a disciplined, steadfast mind.

When you are afraid, remember that God loves you! You

Don't Be Ashamed   45

can discipline your mind and keep it under control by putting your trust in God and His power. You can be loving and kind even when you don't want to, even when you are angry. God has given you power, love, and a sound mind, and you have the potential, the power to use those gifts!

Guided Instruction

1 John 4:11 WHAT are we to do since God loves us? Love one another

1 John 4:18 WHAT do we see about love in this verse? There is no fear in love. Perfect love casts out fear.

2 Timothy 1:7 WHAT else has God given us? D i s c i p l i n e

Isaiah 26:3 HOW do we have a steadfast mind? By trusting in God

Read and discuss the rest of the text for this lesson.

Thank God for the privilege to grow closer to Him.

Guided Instruction

DAY THREE

Ask God to lead you during this study today.

32 Turn to page 45 and read "On Your Mark...Get Set!"

33 Add new key words and how to mark them on your whiteboard or key word bookmark.

Turn to page 160, read 2 Timothy 1:8–14 aloud using your Observation Worksheet visual aid as students follow along and call out each key word. Then mark them together as we noted on p. 13.

Ashamed (draw a brown arch over the word)

Gospel (testimony of our Lord, for which, for this reason, the standard of sound words, and treasure) (draw a red megaphone and color it green)

Suffering (suffer, chains) (draw a red squiggly line)

God (draw a purple triangle and color it yellow)

Christ Jesus (draw a purple cross and color it yellow)

Holy Spirit (draw a purple cloud and color it yellow)

WHEN (draw a green clock over words that denote time)

(page 45)

DAY THREE
ON YOUR MARK...GET SET!

32 "All right, guys." Coach Neighbors called the relay team over. "Are you ready? It is almost time for our relay event. Matthew, remember that a good start is very important. That's why you're our first runner—you're great at getting out of the blocks and off to a quick start. Wes, you're a fast sprinter, and that's why you're next. Josh, you're a great curve runner, and Max, not only are you great under pressure, but you are fast, and we need that fighting spirit to bring that baton over the finish line first! Is everybody ready? Let's get loosened up, but first things first. We need to ask God to give us the strength to do our best and hang in there until the race is finished. Let's pray!"

While the guys are getting ready for the relay event, let's pull out our books. As we have looked at 2 Timothy 1 this week, we have seen that Paul opens his letter to Timothy by encouraging Timothy and affirming him, just as Coach Neighbors encouraged the guys to get them ready for their race. Let's find out WHAT else Paul says in his letter to Timothy.

Turn to page 160. Read 2 Timothy 1:8-14 and mark the key words and the synonyms we have listed for you below. Don't forget to add any new words to your key-word bookmark.

ashamed (draw a brown arch over it like this: ⌒)

gospel (Use the same symbol for any synonyms you

---

46   WEEK TWO

might see. A synonym is a another word that can take the place of the word *gospel* and mean the same thing. If you can put the word *gospel* in the place of this word, then mark it. Here are some examples of synonyms for gospel: *testimony of our Lord* (verse 8), *for which* (verse 11), *for this reason* (verse 12), *the standard of sound words* (verse 13), and *treasure* (verse 14). Draw a red megaphone like this: ◁▷ and color it green.

suffering (suffer, chains) (draw a red squiggly line like this: 〰️)

God (Father) (draw a purple triangle and color it yellow)

Christ Jesus (and any other words that refer to Jesus, like *Lord*) (draw a purple cross and color it yellow)

Holy Spirit (draw a purple ☁ and color it yellow)

(page 46)

Don't forget to mark your pronouns! And mark anything that tells you WHEN by drawing a green clock ⏰ or green circle like this: ◯ .

33 8 Therefore do not be ashamed of the testimony of our Lord or of me His prisoner, but join with me in suffering for the gospel according to the power of God, **35**

9 who has saved us and called us with a holy calling, not according to our works, but according to His own purpose and grace which was granted us in Christ Jesus from all eternity,

10 but now has been revealed by the appearing of our Savior Christ Jesus, who abolished death and brought life and immortality to light through the gospel,

11 for which I was appointed a preacher and an apostle and a teacher.

160

Observation Worksheets—2 Timothy   161

12 For this reason I also suffer these things, but I am not ashamed; for I know whom I have believed and I am convinced that He is able to guard what I have entrusted to Him until that day.

13 Retain the standard of sound words which you have heard from me, in the faith and love which are in Christ Jesus.

14 Guard, through the Holy Spirit who dwells in us, the treasure which has been entrusted to you.

15 Y... away

Don't Be Ashamed   47

Awesome! Did you notice that after Paul encourages Timothy, he gives Timothy some instructions on what Timothy needs to do? An instruction is a specific "do this" or "don't do that" command. Ask the 5 W's and an H to discover WHAT Paul tells Timothy to do.

2 Timothy 1:8 WHAT is the first thing we see Paul telling Timothy *not* to do? _____

Do not be ashamed of the testimony of the Lord or of Paul.

WHAT does Paul mean when he tells Timothy not to be ashamed of the testimony of our Lord? Being ashamed is like fee... someone

Guided Instruction

Reread the selected verses and answer the questions on pages 47-50.

2 Timothy 1:8 WHAT is the first thing we see Paul telling Timothy not to do?
Do not be ashamed of the testimony of the Lord or of Paul.

Guided Instruction

34 Discuss the next three questions and have students respond independently.

Mark 8:38 WHAT will the Son of Man be to the person who is ashamed of Jesus and His words? The <u>Son</u> of <u>Man</u> will also be <u>ashamed</u> of him when He <u>comes</u> in the glory of His Father with the holy angels.

Matthew 10:32-33 WHAT happens if we deny Jesus before men? <u>Jesus will deny us before the Father.</u>

Discuss the next question and have students respond independently.

(page 47)

WHAT does Paul mean when he tells Timothy not to be ashamed of the testimony of our Lord? Being ashamed is like feeling so embarrassed or humiliated that you don't tell someone about Jesus. The phrase "testimony of our Lord" means a witness of Jesus. (Remember, in this passage, this phrase is a synonym that can replace the word *gospel*.) Paul is telling Timothy not to be embarrassed of the gospel of Jesus or of him, the Lord's prisoner.

34 Have you ever felt embarrassed to tell someone about Jesus? _____ WHY? WHAT did you think would happen? _____

_____

HOW do you think Jesus feels about that?

_____

Pull out your official Rulebook, your Bible. Look up and read Mark 8:38 to see WHAT Jesus says about being ashamed of Him.

Mark 8:38 WHAT will the Son of Man be to the person who is ashamed of Jesus and His words?

The ____**Son**____ of ____**Man**____ will also be ____**ashamed**____ of him when He ____**comes**____ in the glory of His Father with the holy angels.

48   WEEK TWO

Look up and read Matthew 10:32-33.

Matthew 10:33 WHAT happens if we deny Jesus before men? **Jesus will deny us before the Father.**

_____

Whoa! That means that if we are ashamed of Jesus and His words while we are living on this earth, He will be ashamed of us when He comes back! He will deny us before God!

Think about that. Have you ever been ashamed of Jesus? Write out what you did or didn't do.

_____

_____

Look up and read 2 Timothy 1:8. WHAT else does Paul tell

(page 48)

Look back at 2 Timothy 1:8. WHAT else does Paul tell Timothy to do?

<u>Join him in suffering for the Gospel</u>

Ouch! That doesn't sound like a lot of fun does it?

2 Timothy 1:8 HOW are we able to suffer like Paul? WHAT does God give us? The p <u>o</u> <u>w</u> <u>e</u> r of God!

Look up and read 1 Corinthians 10:13. HOW is God faithful?

<u>He will not let us be tempted beyond our ability. He will provide a way of escape so that we may endure it.</u>

Suffering isn't fun, but it's part of being a believer in Jesus. When we love and serve Jesus, there will be times of suffering and persecution. Sometimes we will suffer when we don't want to let God run our lives, when we don't want Him to have first

Don't Be Ashamed 49

place. And sometimes we will suffer and be persecuted because of our testimony of believing in Jesus and sharing the gospel with others. People will make fun of us or hurt us. But God is faithful. God will give us a way out of our suffering, or He will give us strength and His power to endure it!

Let's put a green box around each one of the instructions that Paul gives Timothy. Turn to page 160 and put a green box around the instructions *do not be ashamed of the testimony of our Lord or of me His prisoner* and *join with me in suffering for the gospel.*

Do you see any other instructions in verses 8-14? How about in 2 Timothy 1:13? WHAT is Paul's instruction?

<u>Retain the standard of sound words.</u>

2 Timothy 1:14 WHAT does Paul tell Timothy to do?

Guided Instruction

2 Timothy 1:8 WHAT else does Paul tell Timothy to do? <u>Join him in suffering for the Gospel</u>

2 Timothy 1:8 HOW are we able to suffer like Paul? WHAT does God give us? The p <u>o</u> <u>w</u> <u>e</u> r of God

1 Corinthians 10:13 HOW is God faithful? <u>He will not let us be tempted beyond our ability. He will provide a way of escape so that we may endure it.</u>

35 Put a green box around each one of the instructions on page 160. (Teacher Guide page 55)

Do not be ashamed of the testimony of our Lord or of me His prisoner.

Join with me in suffering for the Gospel.

Continue answering the questions about verses 8-14.

2 Timothy 1:13 WHAT is Paul's instruction? <u>Retain the standard of sound words.</u>

Guided Instruction

2 Timothy 1:14 WHAT does Paul tell Timothy to do? <u>Guard the treasure entrusted to you.</u>

HOW are you to guard the treasure? <u>Through the Holy Spirit who dwells in us.</u>

WHAT is the key word marked in each of these instructions? <u>Gospel...Sound words and treasure</u>

36 Complete the list about the Gospel on page 50.

WHAT I Learned About the Gospel

2 Timothy 1:8 Do <u>not</u> be <u>ashamed</u> of the <u>testimony</u> of our <u>Lord</u>.

2 Timothy 1:8 Join with me in <u>suffering</u> for the Gospel.

2 Timothy 1:10 The appearing of our <u>Savior</u> <u>Christ</u> <u>Jesus</u>, who abolished <u>death</u> and brought <u>life</u> and <u>immortality</u> to <u>light</u> through the Gospel.

2 Timothy 1:11 Paul was appointed a <u>preacher</u> and an <u>apostle</u> and a <u>teacher</u> for the Gospel.

(page 49)

2 Timothy 1:14 WHAT does Paul tell Timothy to do?

<u>**Guard the treasure entrusted to you.**</u>

HOW are you to guard the treasure?

Through the _____ **Holy** _____ **Spirit** _____ who
_____ **dwells** _____ in _____ **us** _____.

Wow, the Holy Spirit is going to help you!

Turn to page 161 and draw a green box around each of these instructions in verses 13-14.

Now, WHAT is each one of these instructions to Timothy about? Look at each instruction that you put a green box around on page 161. WHAT is the key word you marked in each of these instructions?

<u>**Gospel...Sound words and treasure**</u>

Amazing! Each one of these instructions is about the gospel! Let's make a list in the box below by looking at each place we

---

50   WEEK TWO

marked *gospel* or any synonyms for the gospel in 2 Timothy 1 on our Observation Worksheet.

36

WHAT I Learned About the Gospel

2 Timothy 1:8 Do __**not**__ be __**ashamed**__ of the __**testimony**__ of our __**Lord**__.

2 Timothy 1:8 Join with me in __**suffering**__ for the gospel.

2 Timothy 1:10 The appearing of our __**Savior**__ __**Christ**__ __**Jesus**__, who abolished __**death**__ and brought __**life**__ and __**immortality**__ to __**light**__ through the gospel.

2 Timothy 1:11 Paul was appointed a __**preacher**__ and an __**apostle**__ and a __**teacher**__ for the gospel.

(page 50)

gospel.

2 Timothy 1:12 Paul ___suffered___ for the gospel but was not ___ashamed___ .

2 Timothy 1:13 ___Retain___ the ___standard___ of ___sound___ ___words___ (the gospel).

2 Timothy 1:14 ___Guard___ the ___treasure___ (the gospel) which has been ___entrusted___ to you.

Wow! Think about what these verses show us about the gospel. We are not to be ashamed of it. We are to suffer for it. It is revealed through Jesus; it is the reason that Paul is a preacher, an

---

Don't Be Ashamed 51

apostle, and a teacher; we are to retain it and guard it; the gospel has been entrusted to us!

You have learned a lot of things about the gospel today, but do you know WHAT the gospel is? Here's a hint. Take a look at verse 10 on your list. Tomorrow you will find out WHAT the gospel is and see WHAT God and Jesus have done for you! You have done a great job! Don't forget to practice your memory verse.

Guided Instruction

2 Timothy 1:12 Paul <u>suffered</u> for the Gospel but was not <u>ashamed</u>.

2 Timothy 1:13 <u>Retain</u> the <u>standard</u> of <u>sound</u> <u>words</u>.

2 Timothy 1:14 <u>Guard</u> the <u>treasure</u> which has been <u>entrusted</u> to you.

Read and discuss the rest of the text in this lesson.

Practice saying the memory verse with a friend.

Guided Instruction

DAY FOUR

Ask God to keep you focused on His Word and give you endurance for this study.

37 Turn to page 51 and read "Pass the Baton."

(page 51)

DAY FOUR

PASS THE BATON!

37 "Great, Matthew, way to go!" Coach Neighbors yelled out as he watched Matthew run in, hit the go mark, and hand the baton off to Wes. "Run, Wes, run! Good, good…now pass that baton to Josh. You got it, Josh! Way to take that curve! Uh-oh…hang in there…get that baton to Max—you can do it. All right, Max, pour it on! You can handle the pressure…push, Max, push!"

---

52   WEEK TWO

"Yeah! You did it! Way to go, guys! Way to go, Josh! You didn't let that turn of the ankle stop you. Way to hang in there and get that baton to Max. You guys are awesome!"

How about that? The guys hung in there. Josh pressed through his pain when he turned his ankle, he was able to hand off the baton to Max, and Max pressed on to win the race! Man, that is so awesome!

Let's find out how we can pass on the baton of the gospel. But before we can pass it on, we need to be sure we know WHAT the gospel is. Don't forget to pray! Then turn to page 160 and read 2 Timothy 1:8–10.

8 Therefore do not be ashamed of the testimony of our Lord or of me His prisoner, but join with me in suffering for the gospel according to the power of God,

38

9 who has saved us and called us with a holy calling, not according to our works, but according to His own purpose and grace which was granted us in Christ Jesus from all eternity,

10 but now has been revealed by the appearing of our Savior Christ Jesus, who abolished death and brought life and immortality to light through the gospel,

11 for which I ~~was appointed a preacher and an apostle and a~~

WHAT is the gospel? Let's ask the 5 W's and an H. *(page 52)*

2 Timothy 1:9 WHAT did God do for us?

He ___saved___ us and ___called___ us with a ___holy___ ___calling___.

2 Timothy 1:9 HOW did God save us?

Not ___according___ to our ___works___ but according to His own ___purpose___ and ___grace___ which was ___granted___ to us in ___Christ Jesus___ from all ___eternity___.

Let's think this through. Grace is something you don't earn. It is something you don't deserve. Grace is a free gift, a total gift.

So are we saved by works—the things we do—or by God's grace—His free gift?

___God's grace___

WHOM is this granted in? ___Christ Jesus___

Don't Be Ashamed 53

Wow! We can do absolutely nothing to save ourselves. It is only through the grace of God. Being saved comes from believing and trusting in Christ Jesus.

2 Timothy 1:10 WHAT did our Savior Christ Jesus do to death?

Jesus ___abolished___ death!

Guided Instruction

38 Reread the selected verses in 2 Timothy 1:8-10 and answer the questions.

2 Timothy 1:9 WHAT did God do for us? He _saved_ us and _called_ us with a _holy calling_.

2 Timothy 1:9 HOW did God save us? Not _according_ to our _works_ but according to His own _purpose_ and _grace_ which was _granted_ to us in _Christ Jesus_ from all _eternity_.

Discuss the next two questions.

2 Timothy 1:10 WHAT did our Savior Christ Jesus do to death? Jesus _abolished_ death!

Guided Instruction

39 Read 1 Corinthians 15:1-8 on page 53 and mark the following key words.

Gospel (draw a red megaphone and color it green)

Christ (draw a purple cross and color it yellow)

Answer the questions about
1 Corinthians 15:1-8.

1 Corinthians 15:1 WHAT is Paul making known to them? WHAT is he preaching? The Gospel

1 Corinthians 15:2-4 WHAT is the Gospel? HOW are you saved? WHAT do you have to believe? Christ died for our sins according to the Scriptures, and that He was buried, and that He was raised on the third day according to the Scriptures.

(page 53)

HOW did Jesus abolish death? Let's read 1 Corinthians 15:1-8 (printed out below) and mark the following key words:

gospel (and any synonyms, like *which* and *the word*) (draw a red megaphone like this: and color it green)

Christ (draw a purple cross and color it yellow)

Don't forget to mark your pronouns!

39

1 Corinthians 15:1-8

1 Now I make known to you, brethren, the gospel which I preached to you, which also you received, in which also you stand, **2** by which also you are saved, if you hold fast the word which I preached to you, unless you believed in vain.

3 For I delivered to you as of first importance what I also received, that Christ died for our sins according to the Scriptures, and that He was buried, **4** and that He was raised on the third day according to the Scriptures, **5** and that He appeared to Cephas, then to the twelve. **6** After that He appeared to more than five hundred brethren at one time, most of whom remain until now, but some have fallen asleep; **7** then He appeared to James, then to all the apostles; **8** and last of all, as to one untimely born, He appeared to me also.

---

54   Week Two

1 Corinthians 15:1 WHAT is Paul making known to them? WHAT is he preaching? The _____Gospel_____

1 Corinthians 15:2-4 WHAT is the gospel? HOW are you saved? WHAT do you have to believe?

_____Christ_____ died for our _____sins_____ according to the _____Scriptures_____ and that He was _____buried_____, and that He was _____raised_____ on the _____third_____ day according to the _____Scriptures_____.

(page 54)

The first point of the gospel is that Jesus died for our sins.

1 Corinthians 15:3 says that Jesus died for our sins according to the Scriptures. This means that Jesus' dying for our sins was written about in the Old Testament before He ever came to earth as a baby. Jesus came to earth as a human being, but He was still God. This is called the *incarnation*. *Incarnation* is a big word that means being or taking flesh. It is God becoming human. Jesus was God in the flesh. This is a very important doctrine (teaching) that is essential to the gospel.

Jesus was different from all other human beings because He was not born a sinner. God was His Father. Although Jesus was tempted like we are, Jesus never sinned. He always obeyed His Father, and because he never sinned, He could pay for our sins.

Jesus' death on the cross was the propitiation (atonement) for our sins. Remember what we learned about propitiation on day 2? *Propitiation* means that God was satisfied with Jesus' payment for our sins.

WHY would Jesus need to pay for our sins? WHAT does sin cause? Look up and read Romans 6:23.

Don't Be Ashamed 55

Romans 6:23 WHAT is the wages of sin?

Death

WHAT is the free gift of God?

Eternal life

Because sin brings death and would separate us from God forever, God in His love for us gave His only Son, Jesus, to die on a cross and to be the propitiation (atonement) for our sins so that we could be with God forever.

Think about it. Jesus, who had never sinned, did not deserve to die, but He chose to take our place and die on the cross to pay for our sin. He was our substitute. His death took away our sins so that we can have the free gift of eternal life! Isn't that incredible!

Look back at 1 Corinthians 15:3 printed out on page 53.

WHAT did people do with Jesus' body after He died?
Buried it

WHY do you bury someone? Because they are dead! So if Jesus was buried, was He really dead? **X** Yes __ No

Guided Instruction

Read and discuss the text at the bottom of page 54

Turn to Romans 6:23 to answer the questions.

Romans 6:23 WHAT is the wages of sin? Death

WHAT is the free gift of God? Eternal life

Return to 1 Corinthians 15 on page 53 and answer the questions.

1 Corinthians 15:3 WHAT did people do with Jesus' body after He died? Buried it

Was He really dead? X Yes

Guided Instruction

1 Corinthians 15:4 WHAT did Jesus do on the third day? He was raised.

Discuss the text on page 55.

1 Corinthians 15:5 WHAT did Jesus do? He appeared to Cephas and the twelve.

1 Corinthians 15:6-8 HOW many others did Jesus appear to? 500, James, all the apostles, and Paul

Read the text and lead a discussion.

Read John 14:6

John 14:6 WHAT does Jesus say? "I am the way, and the truth, and the life; no one comes to the Father but through Me."

Read the rest of the text on page 57 and have students answer the question on page 58 independently.

Practice saying the memory verse with a friend (Teacher Guide page 49).

(page 55)

Is that good news—that Jesus was dead? No! So if dying isn't good news, WHERE is the good news? Look back at 1 Corinthians 15:4 on page 53.

WHAT did Jesus do on the third day?

He was raised.

The second point of the gospel is that Jesus was buried and resurrected.

The good news is that even though Jesus died and was buried, He didn't stay dead—He was raised on the third day!!

---

56   WEEK TWO

HOW do we know that Jesus was raised from the dead? Look at 1 Corinthians 15:5-8.

1 Corinthians 15:5 WHAT did Jesus do?

He appeared to Cephas and the twelve.

1 Corinthians 15:6-8 HOW many others did Jesus appear to?

500, James, all the apostles, and Paul

Do you know WHO the "me" is in verse 8? That's Paul. Jesus appeared to Paul too! Isn't this *amazing*? We know that even though Jesus died, He didn't stay dead. He was raised on the third day! Death could not hold Jesus. Jesus was resurrected—that's how Jesus abolished death and gives us life and immortality. *Immortality* means we will live forever!

So, WHAT is the gospel? The Greek word for *gospel* is *euangelion*. It is pronounced like this: *yoo-ang-ghel-ee-on*. The word *gospel* means "good news." It's the good news that Jesus paid the penalty for our sins. Remember, the payment for sin is death. Sinners have to die, but Jesus didn't *have* to die because He didn't sin. Jesus took our place and *voluntarily* died on the cross so He could pay for our sin! We can't do anything to save ourselves. We can never ever be good enough. Being good does not take away our sins. Jesus is the only one who can take away sin.

Let's look up and read John 14:6.

WHAT does Jesus say? "I am the **way**, and the **truth**, and the **life**; **no one** comes to the **Father** but through **Me**."

WOW! Jesus tells us He is the only way to God! And *no one*—Gentiles, Jews, Hindus, Muslims, Buddhists, or churchgoers—

can get to God without believing in Jesus. Jesus is the *only* way to God and heaven.

This is the gospel. This is the standard of sound words we are to keep and never turn away from, according to 2 Timothy 1:13. This is the treasure we are to guard. It never changes, and it never will. This is why Paul is a prisoner. He believed the gospel. He guarded the truth of it. That's why Paul suffered. Athletes must endure physical suffering and lots of discipline to become champions in their sport, and we must endure suffering and discipline ourselves to become true champions for God.

So HOW do you become God's champion? HOW do you accept Jesus Christ as your Savior and receive eternal life? The first thing you need to do is know WHO Jesus is. You have to believe that Jesus is God's Son, that He is God, and that as a man He lived a perfect life without sin and died on a cross to pay for our sins. Then He was buried, and God raised Him from the dead. He is the *only* Savior!

You have to believe you are a sinner and that you need someone to save you because you can't save yourself. You have to be willing to confess to God that you are a sinner and turn away from your sin (repent). You have to be willing to turn your entire life over to God, to become a follower of Jesus Christ.

If you truly believe in WHO Jesus is and WHAT He did for you, and if you know you are a sinner who cannot save yourself, then you are ready to receive Jesus as your Savior.

To believe in Jesus means you are willing to turn away from doing things your way and to begin obeying Jesus. Jesus puts it this way. You have to be willing to deny yourself, take up your cross (die to being your own God), and follow Him (Mark 8:34).

An athlete has to submit to his coach and learn. In the same way, when you truly believe in Jesus, you are willing to submit to Him and let Him be your Coach, your Boss, your Lord, your Ruler, your God. You have to be willing to let Jesus have complete control over your life.

Take some time and think about what you have learned about WHO Jesus is and WHAT He has done for you. Ask yourself, *Am I ready to give my life to Jesus and let Him take over my life?*

Guided Instruction

58   Week Two

It's a big decision, so think about what it really means. If you aren't sure you understand, you can talk with a grown-up.

All right! Now that you know what the gospel is and how you can receive it, with WHOM can you share the good news about Jesus? _____

_____

Way to go! Now practice your memory verse, and as you say it out loud, think about HOW *awesome* God is and WHAT He has done for you!

(page 58)

DAY FIVE
(40)
FINISH STRONG!

Hey, guys, it's great to have you back on the field for the last day of our track and field events. Are your ready to run a mile for Team USA? It'll take a lot of endurance, but we know you can do it! Sam will run alongside you to encourage you as you run.

Don't Be Ashamed   59

What a race! You won a silver medal. All right! But it could have been gold if you hadn't turned away to look at your opponent. Remember to keep your eyes on the finish line.

Now, catch your breath while you talk to God. Let's head back to 2 Timothy 1. Turn to page 161 and read 2 Timothy 1:15–18. Mark the key words and synonyms listed below.

   ashamed (turned away) (draw a brown arch over it like this:)

   God (Father, Lord) (draw a purple triangle and color it yellow)

Don't forget to mark anything that tells you WHERE by double underlining the WHERE in green. Mark anything that tells you WHEN by drawing a green clock 🕐 or green circle like this: ○ .

   Now, ask those 5 W's and an H to find out who is and who

Guided Instruction

DAY FIVE

This is such a wonderful study. Thank God for the privilege of becoming one of His champions. Ask Him to keep you faithful and help you understand His Word.

40 Turn to page 58 and read "Finish Strong!"

41 Add any new key words to your whiteboard or key word bookmark. Turn to page 161 and read 2 Timothy 1:15-18 aloud as students follow along using your visual aid. Have students call out key words and mark them together, you on your visual aid and they in their books.

Ashamed (turned away) (draw a brown arch over the word)

God (Father, Lord) (draw a purple triangle and color it yellow)

WHERE (double-underline in green words that denote place)

WHEN (draw a green clock over words that denote time)

Reread the selected verses and answer the questions.

Guided Instruction

2 Timothy 1:15 WHO turned away from Paul? All who are in Asia–Phygelus and Hermogenes

Discuss the next three questions and have students respond.

2 Timothy 1:16 WHO was not ashamed of Paul? Onisephorus

2 Timothy 1:16 WHAT did Onesiphorus do for Paul? Refreshed him

2 Timothy 1:17 WHAT did Onesiphorus do when he was in Rome? Found Paul

2 Timothy 1:18 WHAT did Paul ask the Lord to grant Onesiphorus? Mercy from the Lord on that day

(page 161)

41 15 You are aware of the fact that all who are in Asia turned away from me, among whom are Phygelus and Hermogenes.

16 The Lord grant mercy to the house of Onesiphorus, for he often refreshed me and was not ashamed of my chains;

17 but when he was in Rome, he eagerly searched for me and found me—

18 the Lord grant to him to find mercy from the Lord on that day—and you know very well what services he rendered at Ephesus.

(page 59)

Now, ask those 5 W's and an H to find out who is and who isn't ashamed of the gospel.

2 Timothy 1:15 WHO turned away from Paul?

All who are in Asia–Phygelus and Hermogenes

Are you surprised to see that these people turned away, were ashamed of Paul? Do you think that these who are ashamed of Paul are also ashamed of the gospel?

_____

Are they true believers if they are ashamed? _____

From WHAT we have learned, will Jesus confess or deny them? _____

_____

2 Timothy 1:16 WHO was not ashamed of Paul?

Onisephorus

60   WEEK TWO

2 Timothy 1:16 WHAT did Onesiphorus do for Paul?

Refreshed him

2 Timothy 1:17 WHAT did Onesiphorus do when he was in Rome? Found Paul

2 Timothy 1:18 WHAT did Paul ask the Lord to grant Onesiphorus?

Mercy from the Lord on that day

(page 60)

Have you noticed how sometimes kids will be part of a team for a little while but will quit (turn away) when they don't like the coach or the coach is too demanding? Onesiphorus didn't turn away. He was faithful to Paul.

Let's match the people we have met in 2 Timothy 1 in the left column on the next page to the words in the right column by drawing lines to show whether they are ashamed or not ashamed of the gospel.

Think about the things you learned about each one of these people as you studied 2 Timothy 1. For an example, WHAT did you learn about Timothy as you made your lists last week? You saw that Timothy has proven worth, and he has been faithful in serving with Paul in furthering the gospel. So would Timothy be ashamed or not ashamed of the gospel?

_____

Now draw a line from each person's name to show whether they are ashamed or not ashamed of the gospel according to what you have learned about them.

Guided Instruction

Lead a discussion about the text on page 60.

42 Draw a line from each person's name to show whether he was ashamed or not ashamed.

Paul	Not ashamed
Timothy	Not ashamed
All those in Asia	Ashamed
Phygelus	Ashamed
Hermogenes	Ashamed
Onesiphorus	Not ashamed

Read the text on page 61.

Practice saying the memory verse

Thank God for loving you. He sees your perseverance and is pleased.

If you are a classroom teacher you may want to give your students a quiz on their memory verse. There is also a quiz on Week Two on page 156 to check memory and understanding.

This is a great time to review all that the kids have learned in 2 Timothy by playing a game like like *M&M® Draw* on page 165 or the *5W and H Game* on page 166.

Don't Be Ashamed   61

42

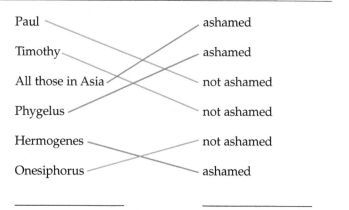

Paul — ashamed
Timothy — ashamed
All those in Asia — not ashamed
Phygelus — not ashamed
Hermogenes — not ashamed
Onesiphorus — ashamed

_____   _____

In the last blank under Onesiphorus' name write your name. Take a moment and ask yourself WHOM you are most like—Paul, Timothy, those in Asia, or Onesiphorus. Then write whom you are most like and what describes you—not ashamed or ashamed of the gospel.

Way to go! You have done an outstanding job this week! Just look at all you have learned. You know how very important the gospel is. You know the gospel is revealed through Jesus, and believing the gospel is the only way you can have eternal life. You know that you are not to be ashamed of it. You know you are to be willing to suffer for it. The gospel is a treasure. You are to keep the truth of it. You are to guard it and share it with others. Awesome! We are so proud of you!

Now take that baton of the gospel and run hard, run fast, and hand it off to your family and friends. Persevere until the race is won! And don't forget to say your memory verse out loud to a grown-up.

Memory Verse

"Who has saved us and called us with a holy calling, not according to our works, but according to His own purpose and grace which was granted us in Christ Jesus from all eternity."

2 Timothy 1:9

Guided Instruction

WEEK 3

DAY ONE

Ask God to lead you during this study.

43 Turn to page 63 and read "2 Timothy 2:1-13" and "Be Strong!"

3

ENTRUST TO FAITHFUL MEN

43

2 TIMOTHY 2:1-13

Last week was incredible as we began competing in our summer games and saw HOW Paul encouraged Timothy in his letter. Paul reminded Timothy of his love for him, the faith they share, and Timothy's need to stir up the gift God gave him. We also saw Paul give Timothy some instructions on his responsibility to the gospel of Jesus Christ. We discovered not only WHAT the gospel is but also HOW important it is for us to pass the gospel on to others.

WHAT will we discover this week? Let's find out.

DAY ONE

BE STRONG!

"Okay, guys." Coach Neighbors gathered the kids together at Hardaway Hall. "You did a great job for Team USA in our track and field events. Tomorrow will begin our swimming and diving events. Girls, the first events are yours. Are you ready to swim for the gold?"

Molly and all the girls gave a loud shout. "All right then!"

63

64   WEEK THREE

Coach smiled. "Let's get our minds prepared by working on 2 Timothy. Molly, why don't you pray so we can see what else Paul has to say to Timothy."

Turn to page 161. Read 2 Timothy 2:1-2 and mark the key words and synonyms listed below.

(page 161)

Chapter 2

44 1 You therefore, my son, be strong in the grace that is in Christ Jesus.

2 The things which you have heard from me in the presence of many witnesses, entrust these to faithful men who will be able to **45** teach others also.

(page 64)

Christ Jesus (and any other words that refer to Jesus, like *Lord*) (draw a purple cross and color it yellow)

gospel (and synonyms for the gospel: *the things which you have heard from me*, and *these* [both in verse 2]) (draw a red megaphone like this: and color it green)

Fantastic! Let's ask the 5 W's and an H to discover Paul's instructions to Timothy.

2 Timothy 2:1 WHAT does Paul tell Timothy to do?

<u>**Be strong in the grace of Jesus**</u>

2 Timothy 2:1 WHERE will Timothy get the strength to do what Paul tells him to do? <u>**In Christ Jesus**</u>

Turn to page 161 and draw a green box around the instruction that Paul gives Timothy in 2 Timothy 2:1.

2 Timothy 2:2 WHAT are "the things which you have heard"?

The g <u>o</u> <u>s</u> <u>p</u> <u>e</u> <u>l</u>

2 Timothy 2:2 WHAT is Paul's instruction about the gospel?

<u>**Entrust it to faithful men.**</u>

2 Timothy 2:2 WHY did Paul say Timothy was to entrust the gospel to faithful men? WHAT kind of men

---

Guided Instruction

44 Turn to page 161 and read 2 Timothy 2:1-2 aloud using your Observation Worksheet visual aid as students follow along and call out each key word. Then mark them together as we noted on p. 13.

Christ Jesus (draw a purple cross and color it yellow)

Gospel and synonyms (draw a red megaphone and color it green)

Answer the questions about Paul's instructions to Timothy.

2 Timothy 2:1 WHAT does Paul tell Timothy to do? <u>Be strong in the grace of Jesus</u>

2 Timothy 2:1 WHERE will Timothy get the strength to do what Paul tells him to do? <u>In Christ Jesus</u>

45 Turn to page 161 and draw a green box around the instructions Paul gives Timothy in 2 Timothy 2:1.

2 Timothy 2:2 WHAT are "the things which you have heard"? The G <u>o</u> <u>s</u> <u>p</u> <u>e</u> <u>l</u>

2 Timothy 2:2 WHAT is Paul's instruction about the Gospel? <u>Entrust it to faithful men.</u>

Guided Instruction

2 Timothy 2:2 WHY did Paul say Timothy was to entrust the Gospel to faithful men? WHAT kind of men did we see in 2 Timothy 1:15, faithful men or unfaithful? Unfaithful

2 Timothy 1:16-18 HOW about Onesiphorus—was he faithful or unfaithful? Faithful

2 Timothy 2:2 WHAT will these faithful men be able to do? Teach others

Read and discuss the text on page 65.

Entrust to Faithful Men 65

did we see in 2 Timothy 1:15, faithful men or unfaithful? **Unfaithful**

2 Timothy 1:16-18 HOW about Onesiphorus—was he faithful or unfaithful? **Faithful**

2 Timothy 2:2 WHAT will these faithful men be able to do?

Teach others

Turn to page 159. Draw a green box around the instruction that Paul gives Timothy in 2 Timothy 2:2.

To be able to teach someone God's Word, you have to learn it yourself. You're doing that right now! But it doesn't stop there. You need not only to know it but also to help others learn it. And HOW do you do that? One way you can teach others is to ask your friends if they would like to do one of these Bible studies with you. Do you know of someone you could ask to do a study with you? Write his or her name here: _____ .

Pray and ask God to give your friends the desire to study His Word with you, and ask Him to help you show them how to see truth for themselves.

All right! You are doing great! Take a look at the swimming pool on the next page to solve your memory verse. Each of the swimming lanes contains different words. Some of these words have to do with swimming. Look at each word, and if it has to do with swimming, put an X over it. Then write all the unmarked words on the blanks underneath to solve your verse. Read 2 Timothy 2 to find the reference for this verse.

Guided Instruction

46 Solve the memory verse on page 66.

Be diligent to present yourself approved to God as a workman who does not need to be ashamed, accurately handling the word of truth.
2 Timothy 2:15

Copy the memory verse to an index card and practice saying it three times, three times each day.

---

66   WEEK THREE

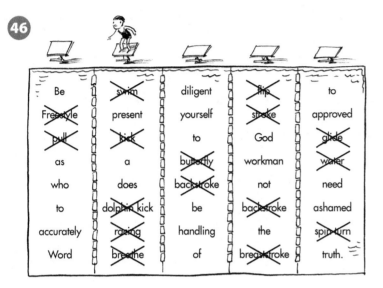

Be	swim	diligent	flip	to
Freestyle	present	yourself	stroke	approved
pull	kick	to	God	glide
as	a	butterfly	workman	water
who	does	backstroke	not	need
to	dolphin kick	be	backstroke	ashamed
accurately	racing	handling	the	spin turn
Word	breathe	of	breaststroke	truth.

Be   diligent   to   present
yourself   approved   to   God
as   a   workman   who   does
not   need   to   be   ashamed,
accurately   handling   the
word   of   truth.

2 Timothy 2: 15

Now, write this verse out and practice saying it out loud three times in a row!

Guided Instruction

DAY TWO

Ask God for clear focus and perseverance as you study His Word today.

47 Turn to page 67 and read "Compete to Win."

DAY TWO
COMPETE TO WIN

47

"Molly, Katie, Morgan, and Bethany, it's almost time for the 400-meter freestyle relay," Coach Neighbors told the girls as they gathered at the pool. "Now, just remember the rules," he continued. "Don't forget to touch the wall so the next swimmer can dive in, and make sure you don't dive into the pool until your teammate has touched the wall, or you will be disqualified. Remember, you disqualify yourself when you don't follow the rules. Are you girls ready? Shake those arms to loosen up."

While the girls are warming up for their event, let's work on our letter from Paul. Pray and ask God to help you to be strong and entrust the gospel to others.

All right! Now, turn to page 161. Read 2 Timothy 2:3-6 and mark the key words listed below (and any synonyms).

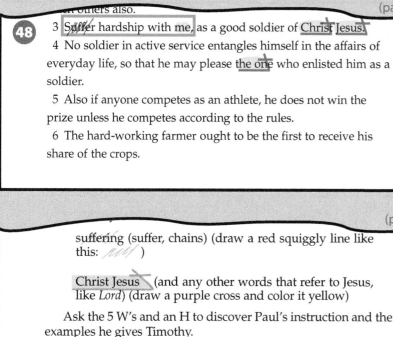

(page 161)

48 3 Suffer hardship with me, as a good soldier of Christ Jesus.

4 No soldier in active service entangles himself in the affairs of everyday life, so that he may please the one who enlisted him as a soldier.

5 Also if anyone competes as an athlete, he does not win the prize unless he competes according to the rules.

6 The hard-working farmer ought to be the first to receive his share of the crops.

(page 68)

suffering (suffer, chains) (draw a red squiggly line like this: ///////)

Christ Jesus (and any other words that refer to Jesus, like *Lord*) (draw a purple cross and color it yellow)

Ask the 5 W's and an H to discover Paul's instruction and the examples he gives Timothy.

2 Timothy 2:3 WHAT is Paul's instruction to Timothy?

_____**Suffer**_____ _____**hardship**_____ with me.

Turn to page 161 and draw a green box around the instruction that Paul gives Timothy.

2 Timothy 2:3 HOW does Paul tell Timothy to suffer hardship with him? WHAT is his example?

Like a good _____**soldier**_____ of _____**Christ**_____
_____**Jesus**_____.

2 Timothy 2:4 WHAT do we learn about the soldier? WHAT kind of service is he in? _____**Active**_____
_____**service**_____

2 Timothy 2:4 WHAT doesn't the soldier in active service do?

_____**Entangle**_____ himself in the _____**affairs**_____
of _____**every**_____ _____**day**_____.

2 Timothy 2:4 WHAT does the soldier want to do?

_____**Please**_____ the one who _____**enlisted**_____ him
as a soldier.

Guided Instruction

48 Turn to page 161 and read 2 Timothy 2:3-6 aloud using your Observation Worksheet visual aid as students follow along and call out each key word. Then mark them together as we noted on p. 13.

Suffering (suffer, chains) (draw a red squiggly line)

Christ Jesus (draw a purple cross and color it yellow)

Read the selected verses to answer the questions.

2 Timothy 2:3 WHAT is Paul's instruction to Timothy? Suffer hardship with me.

Turn to page 161 and draw a green box around the instructions.

2 Timothy 2:3 HOW does Paul tell Timothy to suffer hardship with him? WHAT is his example? Like a good soldier of Christ Jesus

2 Timothy 2:4 WHAT do we learn about the soldier? WHAT kind of service is he in? Active service

2 Timothy 2:4 WHAT doesn't the soldier in active service do? Entangle himself in the affairs of every day

2 Timothy 2:4 WHAT does the soldier want to do? Please the one who enlisted him as a soldier

Guided Instruction

49 Lead a discussion about the text on page 69.

2 Timothy 2:5 WHAT is our example?
An <u>athlete</u>

2 Timothy 2:5 WHAT do we learn about the athlete? He does not <u>win</u> the <u>prize</u> unless he competes according to the <u>rules</u>.

Look up the selected Scripture to answer the questions about athletes.

1 Corinthians 9:24 WHAT is the athlete to do? <u>Run</u> in such a way that you may <u>win</u>.

Entrust to Faithful Men   69

49   A good soldier knows he is to give his undivided allegiance to please the one he serves. He does not get caught up in everyday life. He knows his duties, and he keeps his focus on what he is called to do. A good soldier never runs away from the front lines, even when the battle is fierce. He stands his ground and continues to fight because of something he is willing to suffer for, something worth living and dying for.

Do you want to be a good soldier? Is it the desire of your heart to please God? _____. Write out one way you can please God. _____

WHAT can you do to keep yourself from getting caught up in the world you live in? Will you be careful about the clothes you wear, the music you listen to, and the movies you see so that you please God and not your friends? Write out WHAT you will do to keep yourself from getting entangled in this world.

_____

_____

Now, what is the next example that Paul gives us? Look at 2 Timothy 2:5 WHAT is our example?

An _____**athlete**_____

2 Timothy 2:5 WHAT do we learn about the athlete?

He does not _____**win**_____ the _____**prize**_____ unless he competes according to the _____**rules**_____.

How about that? An athlete's life is about obedience. If he doesn't follow the rules, he won't get the prize. Remember what Coach Neighbors told the girls about touching the wall.

Look up and read 1 Corinthians 9:24-27.

1 Corinthians 9:24 WHAT is the athlete to do?

_____**Run**_____ in such a way that you may _____**win**_____.

70   WEEK THREE

1 Corinthians 9:25 WHAT does the one who competes in the games have to exercise? ____**Self**____- ____**control**____ in all things.

An athlete's life is about self-control and obedience. He disciplines his body so he can compete in the games. If he doesn't obey the rules, he will be disqualified, and he won't win the prize! Don't you want to be the best you can be for God? Write out a way you will discipline yourself. HOW will you obey God?

_____

_____

Did you also notice that 1 Corinthians 9:25 says the athlete wins a perishable prize, one that won't last, but we receive an imperishable prize, one that lasts forever? In 2 Timothy 4:7-8 we read about a reward for finishing the course. Did you know that there are rewards for loving and serving God? Look up and read Revelation 22:12.

Revelation 22:12 WHAT does Jesus have with Him when He comes?

His ____**rewards**____

WHOM is He going to give this to?

Every ___**man**___ according to what he has __**done**__

Wow! Even though we are saved by grace and not by the things we do, the things we do are important. Our actions don't save us, but they show that we love and serve God. One day we will receive a reward!

Let's look at our last example.

2 Timothy 2:6 WHOM does Paul give us as an example?

The ___**hard**___-___**working**___ ___**farmer**___

Guided Instruction

1 Corinthians 9:25 WHAT does the one who competes in the games have to exercise? Self-control in all things

Read and discuss the text. Then read the selected scripture about rewards.

Revelation 22:12 WHAT does Jesus have with Him when He comes? His rewards

WHOM is He going to give this to? Every man according to what he has done.

2 Timothy 2:6 WHOM does Paul give us as an example? The hard-working farmer

Guided Instruction

2 Timothy 2:6 WHAT will he be the first to receive? His <u>share</u> of the <u>crops</u>

Read and discuss the rest of the text on page 71.

Practice saying the memory verse with a friend (Teacher Guide page 73).

Entrust to Faithful Men   71

2 Timothy 2:6 WHAT will he be the first to receive?

His _____**share**_____ of the ____**crops**____

The farmer works hard. He has to get up early to plow, sow, tend, and reap his harvest. He has trials—like bugs, frost, and droughts—that can destroy his crops. But a farmer who works hard and endures will reap a harvest.

Are you willing to work hard for God? _____

WHAT are some trials you might face as you serve Him?

_____

Do you know any kids who don't have to work for anything, who don't have any responsibilities? We are to be like the farmer. We are to work hard and endure. Being a Christian is not a free ride.

If you share the Word (plant the seed) so others can know about Jesus, and if you endure by working hard, being faithful, and not giving up, you will get to share in the harvest, just as the farmer does. Remember, Jesus is coming back one day soon, and His reward is with Him. Will you hang in there and endure so you can reap a harvest?

Aren't these awesome examples? Paul has mentioned the good soldier, the athlete, and the farmer to show us that becoming a champion for God requires suffering, undivided allegiance, self-discipline, obedience, hard work, and endurance.

Don't forget to practice your memory verse!

Guided Instruction

DAY THREE

RECEIVE THE PRIZE

Max, Matthew, Wes, and Josh all cheered as the girls lined up on the platform to receive their prize for the 400-meter freestyle relay. "Way to go, girls, you did great!" They whistled and clapped as each girl was awarded a gold medal.

Aren't you proud of our awesome team? Those girls disciplined themselves to keep their cool under all that pressure. They worked so hard and didn't give up, and now just look—they have won gold medals! Remember, if we don't work, we won't receive a reward.

How about you? Are you ready to work hard so you can receive God's reward? Don't forget to ask God for His help so you can discipline yourself to please Him.

Now, turn to page 162. Read 2 Timothy 2:7-10 and mark the key words listed below (and any synonyms).

---

162   *Observation Worksheets*

 7 Consider what I say, for the Lord will give you understanding in everything.

8 Remember Jesus Christ, risen from the dead, descendant of David, according to my gospel,

9 for which I suffer hardship even to imprisonment as a criminal; but the word of God is not imprisoned.

10 For this reason I endure all things for the sake of those who are chosen, so that they also may obtain the salvation which is in Christ Jesus and with it eternal glory.

11 I...

(page 72)

God (Father) (draw a purple triangle and color it yellow)

Christ Jesus (and any other words that refer to Jesus, like *Lord*) (draw a purple cross and color it yellow)

gospel (and synonyms for the gospel: *for which, the word of God* [verse 9], *for this reason* [verse 10]) (draw a red megaphone like this: and color it green)

suffering (suffer, chains) (draw a red squiggly line like this:)

DAY THREE

Ask God to give you clear understanding of His special message today.

50 Turn to page 72 and read "Receive the Prize."

51 Turn to page 162 and read 2 Timothy 2:7-10 aloud using your Observation Worksheet visual aid as students follow along and call out each key word. Then mark them together as we noted on p. 13.

God (Father) (draw a purple triangle and color it yellow)

Christ Jesus (draw a purple cross and color it yellow)

Suffering (draw a red squiggly line)

Guided Instruction

Read the selected verses to answer the questions.

2 Timothy 2:7 WHAT is Paul's next instruction? <u>Consider</u> what I <u>say</u>.

52 Turn to page 162 and draw a green box around this instruction (Teacher Guide page 79).

2 Timothy 2:7 WHEN you consider what Paul says, when you think on these things, WHAT will the LORD give you? <u>Understanding</u> in everything

2 Timothy 2:8 WHAT is the next instruction? <u>Remember</u> <u>Jesus</u> <u>Christ</u>

53 Turn to page 162 and draw a green box around this instruction (Teacher Guide page 79).

2 Timothy 2:8 WHY are we to remember? WHAT did Jesus do for us? Jesus Christ is <u>risen</u> from the <u>dead</u>.

2 Timothy 2:8 WHO is Jesus? A <u>descendant</u> of <u>David</u>

2 Timothy 2:9 WHAT is not imprisoned? The <u>word</u> of <u>God</u>

2 Timothy 2:10 WHY is Paul enduring all things? For the g <u>o</u> s p e <u>l</u>, for the sake of those who are <u>chosen</u>, so that they may obtain <u>salvation</u>.

(page 72)

2 Timothy 2:7 WHAT is Paul's next instruction?

_____Consider_____ what I ___say___.

Paul wants Timothy to think on these things.

Entrust to Faithful Men   73

Turn to page 162 and draw a green box around this instruction.

2 Timothy 2:7 WHEN you consider what Paul says, when you think on these things, WHAT will the Lord give you?
___Understanding___ in everything

2 Timothy 2:8 WHAT is the next instruction?
___Remember___   ___Jesus___   ___Christ___.

Turn to page 162 and draw a green box around this instruction.

2 Timothy 2:8 WHY are we to remember? WHAT did Jesus do for us? Jesus Christ is ___risen___ from the ___dead___.

Jesus conquered death for us!

2 Timothy 2:8 WHO is Jesus?

A ___descendant___ of ___David___

2 Timothy 2:9 Even though we are suffering and even imprisoned, WHAT is not imprisoned?

The ___word___ ___of___ ___God___

2 Timothy 2:10 WHY is Paul enduring all things?

For the g _o_ _s_ _p_ _e_ _l_, for the sake of those who are ___chosen___, so that they may obtain ___salvation___

Way to go! God's Word is never imprisoned. We are to be like a good soldier, athlete, and farmer. We are to give God first place, please Him, obey His commands, suffer hardship, and endure so that others may receive salvation in Christ Jesus!

Guided Instruction

54 Go back and find all words in each blank. Circle each one in the word search on page 74.

Good job. God sees and is pleased with your desire to know Him.

---

74 WEEK THREE

Now go back and find all the words in each blank starting on page 68 on day 2 and going through today's questions (not including your application questions) and circle each one of these words in the word search below. (If a word is used more than once, circle it just one time.)

You have done an outstanding job! What a way to please God!

54

Guided Instruction

DAY FOUR

Ask God to give you clear focus as you learn how to draw closer to Him.

55 Turn to page 75 and read "Dive Into Truth."

56 Turn to page 162 and read 2 Timothy 2:11-13 aloud using your Observation Worksheet visual aid as students follow along and call out the key word below. Then mark them together as we noted on p. 13.

Christ Jesus (draw a purple cross and color it yellow)

Answer the following questions.

2 Timothy 2:11 WHAT is this statement? A <u>trustworthy</u> statement

WHAT is the first part of this true statement? For if we <u>died</u> with <u>Him</u>

2 Timothy 2:11 WHO is the Him? <u>Christ Jesus</u>

Read Romans 6:3-10 to answer the questions about our old self.

Romans 6:6 WHAT do we see about our old self? <u>We are crucified with Jesus.</u>

Entrust to Faithful Men   75

DAY FOUR
DIVE INTO TRUTH

55   Amazing! That was smoothest dive we have ever seen you do. You sliced right into that pool with hardly a splash! Another gold medal for Team USA! Wasn't it a little bit nerve-racking as you climbed up each one of those steps and looked off the diving platform? All that training sure paid off. Why don't you dry off so we can find out about a trustworthy statement Paul mentions in his letter. Don't forget to pray!

Turn to page 162 so we can dive into God's Word. Read 2 Tim... ...mark the following key word...

(page 162)

...st jesus and with it eternal glory.

56 11 It is a trustworthy statement:
For if we died with <u>Him</u>, we will also live with <u>Him</u>;
12 If we endure, we will also reign with <u>Him</u>;
If we deny <u>Him</u>, <u>He</u> also will deny us;
13 If we are faithless, <u>He</u> remains faithful, for <u>He</u> cannot deny <u>Himself</u>.
14 B...

(page 75)

<u>Christ Jesus</u> (draw a purple cross and color it yellow)

Now, ask the 5 W's and an H.

2 Timothy 2:11 WHAT is this statement?

A _____**trustworthy**_____ statement

That means that it is a true statement. WHAT is the first part of this true statement in 2 Timothy 2:11?

For if we _____**died**_____ with _____**Him**_____

2 Timothy 2:11 WHO is the *Him*? Look back at verse 10 to see WHO this *Him* is. Salvation is in WHOM? _____

_____**Christ Jesus**_____

Look up and read Romans 6:3-10.

Romans 6:6 WHAT do we see about our old self?

_____**We are crucified with Jesus.**_____

76   WEEK THREE

WHY? In order that our body of ___**sin**___ might be done away with, so that we would no longer be ___**slaves**___ to ___**sin**___.

To die with Christ is to surrender our lives to Jesus by accepting Jesus as our Lord and Savior, confessing our sin, and changing the way we live. We have died to our old self. We are no longer slaves to sin. By dying to sin, we identify ourselves with Jesus' death.

So, WHAT is the second part of the true statement?

2 Timothy 2:11 WHAT happens if we die with Christ?

We will ___**live**___ with Him.

Look back at Romans 6:9-10.

Romans 6:9 WHAT do we see about Christ?

He was raised from the dead.

Romans 6:9 WHAT do we see about death?

It is no longer master over Him.

Isn't that *awesome*? Because Jesus was resurrected, death no longer has any hold on Him. And when we identify ourselves with Jesus and give Him our lives, death doesn't have a hold on us either! When we die, we will be raised—just like Jesus—to live with Him forever!

Look at Romans 6:10 WHAT did Christ do?

He ___**died**___ to ___**sin**___ once for all; but the ___**life**___ that He ___**lives**___, He ___**lives**___ to ___**God**___.

Did you catch this last part in verse 10? HOW does Christ live?

To God

Guided Instruction

WHY? **In order that our body of <u>sin</u> might be done away with, so that we would no longer be <u>slaves</u> to <u>sin</u>.**

WHAT is the second part of the true statement?

2 Timothy 2:11 WHAT happens if we die in Christ? We will <u>live</u> with Him.

Romans 6:9 WHAT do we see about Christ? <u>He was raised from the dead.</u>

Romans 6:9 WHAT do we see about death? <u>It is no longer master over Him.</u>

Romans 6:10 WHAT did Christ do? He <u>died</u> to <u>sin</u> once for all; but the <u>life</u> that He <u>lives</u>, He <u>lives</u> to <u>God</u>.

Read the rest of the questions on page 77 and have students respond

Practice saying the memory verse with a friend (Teacher Guide page 73).

Guided Instruction

Entrust to Faithful Men   77

Because Jesus gave up His life for us, we will live with Jesus forever! Isn't that exciting! We have been saved from our death and sin, and now we are to live our lives for God!

Are you doing that? Think about HOW you spend your time. Write out HOW you spend your time every day.

_____

_____

Do these things show that you are living your life for God, or are these just things you want to do?

_____

HOW can you live your life for God? WHAT kinds of things do you think God would like you to spend your time doing?

_____

Do you ask God how you can live for Him? Write out a prayer to God on the lines below and ask Him HOW you can live your life for Him. _____

_____

_____

_____

HOW can you give your best to God? Could God want you to be willing to reach out and serve other people to show His love to them? Read each one of the statements below and put a checkmark by the ones you will do.

- I will reach out and be a friend to someone in my school or at church who is shy or needs a friend. _____
- I will work hard at school and do my best instead of goofing off and just getting by. _____

---

78   WEEK THREE

- I will use my talents to play sports, a musical instrument, or serve others. _____
- I will help my mom and dad at home. _____
- I will help someone else, like a neighbor or an older lady who may need help working in her yard, cutting grass, or cleaning house. _____

All right! Think about the talents you have and use them for God. Tomorrow we will continue to look at the trustworthy statements that Paul tells Timothy about. Don't forget to practice your memory verse!

DAY FIVE

57 ## ENDURE TO THE END

"Sam, come back here. Sam, don't you jump in that pool!" Max yelled out as he chased Sam. "Hey, Molly, run around the pool on the other side. Let's see if we can catch Sam before he hits the water."

Splash! Too late. Sam, you are one bad dog! What are we ever going to do with you? Why don't you dry Sam off so Max and

Matthew get can get ready for the boys' last swimming event. Grab your towel and your book, and let's head back to 2 Timothy 2. Don't forget to pray.

Turn to page 162 and read 2 Timothy 2:11-13. WHAT is the next part of the true statement that Paul makes to Timothy?

(page 162)

58 11 It is a trustworthy statement:
For if we died with Him, we will also live with Him;
12 If we endure, we will also reign with Him;
If we deny Him, He also will deny us;
13 If we are faithless, He remains faithful, for He cannot deny Himself.
14 B

(page 78)

Guided Instruction

DAY FIVE

Ask God to give you full understanding of His Word.

57 Turn to page 78 and read "Endure to the End."

58 Turn to page 162 and read 2 Timothy 2:11-13. WHAT is the next part of the true statement?

Guided Instruction

2 Timothy 2:12 WHAT happens if we endure? We will reign with Him.

Read the selected verses from James and Revelation to answer the next questions.

James 1:12 WHAT will the man receive who perseveres under trial? The crown of life

Revelation 20:4-6 WHAT do we see about those who have a part in the first resurrection? WHAT will they be? Priests of God and of Christ

WHAT will they do? Reign with Him for 1,000 years

What is the next part of the true statement?

2 Timothy 2:12 WHAT happens if we deny Jesus? He will deny us.

How can we deny Jesus? Look up Titus 1:16.

Titus 1:16 WHAT do they profess? To know God

Titus 1:16 HOW do they deny God? By their deeds

Titus 1:16 HOW are they described? Detestable, disobedient, worthless

Lead a discussion about the next two questions.

(page 79)

2 Timothy 2:12 WHAT happens if we endure?

__We will reign with Him.__

Look up and read James 1:12.

WHAT will the man receive who perseveres under a trial?
__The crown of life__

Look up and read Revelation 20:4-6.

Revelation 20:6 WHAT do we see about those who have a part in the first resurrection. WHAT will they be?

__Priests__ of God and of __Christ__

WHAT will they do?
__Reign with Him for 1,000 years__

Isn't that amazing? If we hang in there and persevere, one day we will reign with Christ! Christianity isn't for quitters! Let's look at the next part of our true statement.

2 Timothy 2:12 WHAT happens if we deny Jesus?

__He will deny us.__

HOW can we deny Jesus? Look up and read Titus 1:16.

Titus 1:16 WHAT do they profess?
__To know God__

---

80   WEEK THREE

Titus 1:16 HOW do they deny God?
__By their deeds__

Titus 1:16 HOW are they described?
__Detestable, disobedient, worthless__

WOW! Once again we see that the things we do show whether or not we really know God. Are you obedient or disobedient?

_____

WHAT are your deeds? WHAT are the things you do that show that you love and serve God? _____

_____

2:12 WHAT _____ if _____ ___ faith-

(page 80)

Look at 2 Timothy 2:13 WHAT happens if we are faithless?

__He remains faithful.__

WHY will He remain faithful?

__He cannot deny Himself.__

God is soooooo *awesome*! Even when we lack faith and are unfaithful, He is still faithful! God is always true to Himself. Isn't that exciting? We can always trust God because He is ALWAYS faithful. God always acts according to His character and His promises.

You have learned so much this week in 2 Timothy 2, and we aren't even finished yet. Don't forget to say your memory verse to a grown-up. This is a very important verse that we will take a closer look at next week. Now, go celebrate Max and Matthew's great 100-meter swim!

Guided Instruction

2 Timothy 2:13 WHAT happens if we are faithless? He remains faithful.

WHY will He remain faithful? He cannot deny Himself.

Practice saying the memory verse with a friend.

Good Job! You have persevered!

If you are a classroom teacher you may want to give your students a quiz on their memory verse. There is also a quiz on Week Three on page 157 to check memory and understanding.

If you are a Sunday School teacher this is a great time to review all that the kids have learned in 2 Timothy by playing a game.

Memory Verse

"Be diligent to present yourself approved to God as a workman who does not need to be ashamed, accurately handling the word of truth."

2 Timothy 2:15

Guided Instruction

WEEK 4

DAY ONE

Ask God to be with you during this study. He will guide you to understanding.

59 Turn to page 81 and read "2 Timothy 2:14-26" and "Hit the Mat!"

60 Turn to page 161 and reread 2 Timothy 2:1-13 to find descriptions of a true believer.

4

HANDLE GOD'S WORD ACCURATELY

59

2 TIMOTHY 2:14-26

Wasn't competing in our swimming events fun? As we dove a little deeper into 2 Timothy 2, we saw some amazing examples: the good soldier, the athlete, and the farmer. We discovered that to be a true champion for God, we need to give God first place in our lives, please Him, obey His commands, suffer hardship, and endure to the end. Then we will be sure to receive the prize. And we saw that we are saved by grace in Christ Jesus, but our deeds show whether we are true believers in Jesus.

WHAT will we uncover as we continue in 2 Timothy 2? Let's head to the gym and find out. We need to get ready for our gymnastic events.

DAY ONE
HIT THE MAT!

"Good work, Molly, that was a great front walkover." Coach Neighbors patted Molly on the back as she finished her floor exercise. "Katie, you're up next." Katie took a deep breath as the music started and she began her routine.

81

Guided Instruction

"Fantastic, girls, I think we're ready for tomorrow. Why don't you clean up—we going to meet the boys at Hardaway Hall to work on 2 Timothy."

Today, let's put ourselves back in the context of 2 Timothy 2. We want to see what characteristics we can discover in 2 Timothy 2:1-13 that describe a faithful follower of Jesus. Don't forget to talk to God!

Turn to page 161 and read 2 Timothy 2:1-13. The characteristics of a true believer listed below are from these verses. Draw a line from the first part of the statement on the left to the statement that it matches on the right.

(page 161)

Chapter 2

1 You therefore, my son, be strong in the grace that is in Christ Jesus.

2 The things which you have heard from me in the presence of many witnesses, entrust these to faithful men who will be able to teach others also.

3 Suffer hardship with me, as a good soldier of Christ Jesus.

4 No soldier in active service entangles himself in the affairs of everyday life, so that he may please the one who enlisted him as a soldier.

5 Also if anyone competes as an athlete, he does not win the prize unless he competes according to the rules.

6 The hard-working farmer ought to be the first to receive his share of the crops.

162 *Observation Worksheets*

7 Consider what I say, for the Lord will give you understanding in everything.

8 Remember Jesus Christ, risen from the dead, descendant of David, according to my gospel,

9 for which I suffer hardship even to imprisonment as a criminal; but the word of God is not imprisoned.

10 For this reason I endure all things for the sake of those who are chosen, so that they also may obtain the salvation which is in Christ Jesus and with it eternal glory.

11 It is a trustworthy statement:
For if we died with Him, we will also live with Him;

12 If we endure, we will also reign with Him;
If we deny Him, He also will deny us;

13 If we are faithless, He remains faithful, for He cannot deny Himself.

14

Guided Instruction

61 On page 82, match the first part of statement on the left to the statements on the right.

Entrust the gospel	to faithful men
Suffer	hardship
Active	service
Does not entangle himself	in affairs of everyday life
Pleases the one who	enlisted him
Competes according to	the rules
Wins the	prize
Endures	all things
Died with	Christ
If we endure	we will reign with Him

Look at 2 Timothy 2:12. WHAT part of the true statement describes an unbeliever? <u>Deny Christ</u>

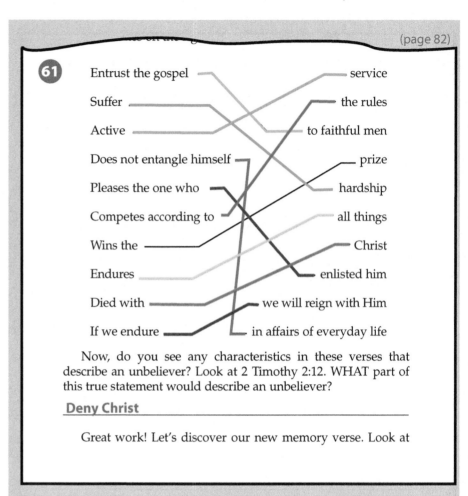

(page 82)

61

Entrust the gospel — service

Suffer — the rules

Active — to faithful men

Does not entangle himself — prize

Pleases the one who — hardship

Competes according to — all things

Wins the — Christ

Endures — enlisted him

Died with — we will reign with Him

If we endure — in affairs of everyday life

Now, do you see any characteristics in these verses that describe an unbeliever? Look at 2 Timothy 2:12. WHAT part of this true statement would describe an unbeliever?

<u>**Deny Christ**</u>

Great work! Let's discover our new memory verse. Look at

Handle God's Word Accurately   83

the exercise mat in the gym on the next page. Coach Neighbors has taped some letters in squares on our mat to help us exercise our mind and discover our new memory verse.

Look at the pair of letters and numbers under each blank. Then go to the exercise mat and find the letter such as A on the right side of the mat, and then go up until you find the number that goes with the A such as 4. Find the letter in the square that goes with A4 and fill it in on the blank. Do the same thing for each blank until you have discovered your verse for the week.

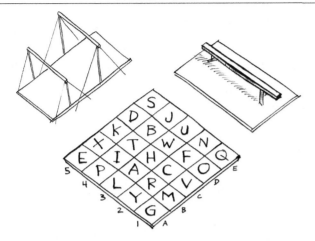

84   WEEK FOUR

62 Now flee from

E2 D1 D3 D2 A3 A5 A5 D2 B2 D1 B1

youthful lusts and

A2 D1 E3 C4 C3 D2 E3 A3 A3 E3 E5 C4 E5 B3 E2 D5

pursue righteousness,

A4 E3 B2 E5 E3 A5 B2 B4 A1 C3 C4 A5 D1 E3 E5 E2 A5 E5 E5

faith, love and peace,

D2 B3 B4 C4 C3 A3 D1 C1 A5 B3 E2 D5 A4 A5 B3 C2 A5

with those who call

D3 B4 C4 C3 C4 C3 D1 E5 A5 D3 C3 D1 C2 B3 A3 A3

on the Lord with a

D1 E2 C4 C3 A5 A3 D1 B2 D5 D3 B4 C4 C3 B3

pure heart.

A4 E3 B2 A5 C3 A5 B3 B2 C4

2 Timothy 2: **22**

Handle God's Word Accurately   85

All right! Don't forget to write your verse out and practice saying it out loud three times today!

Guided Instruction

62 Follow the directions to decipher the memory verse on page 84.

Now flee from youthful lusts and pursue righteousness, faith, love and peace, with those who call on the Lord with a pure heart.

2 Timothy 2:22

Copy the memory verse to an index card and practice saying it three times, three times a day.

Guided Instruction

DAY TWO

Ask God to give you clarity while studying His Word today.

63 Turn to page 85 and read "Flip for God!"

(page 85)

DAY TWO
FLIP FOR GOD!

63 "Man, that was awesome!" Max turned to Matthew. "Did you see those handsprings and backflips? I never knew Katie could flip like that!"

"Look, Max, here comes her score." Josh punched Max. "Man, she got three 9s! Katie got three 9s! All right! Go Team USA!"

Wes looked at Max. "Molly's up next."

"Here she comes," Josh said, "and there she goes." All the guys laughed at Josh's craziness as Molly started her floor exercise. "Man," Josh exclaimed. "I hope we do as well as the girls are. Look—here comes Molly's score…she got a 9, another 9, and an 8.8. Katie got the gold, and Molly got the silver. Way to go, girls!"

All right! How did you like competing in the floor exercise? Even though it is a lot of hard work, we are having so much fun!

---

86   WEEK FOUR

Let's head back to 2 Timothy 2. Don't forget to talk to God, our heavenly Coach!

Turn to page 162. Read 2 Timothy 2:14-21 and mark the key words listed below (and any synonyms).

(page 162)

64 14 Remind them of these things, and solemnly charge them in the presence of God not to wrangle about words, which is useless and leads to the ruin of the hearers.

15 Be diligent to present yourself approved to God as a workman who does not need to be ashamed, accurately handling the word of truth. **65**

16 But avoid worldly and empty chatter, for it will lead to further ungodliness, **66**

17 and their talk will spread like gangrene. Among them are Hymenaeus and Philetus,

18 men who have gone astray from the truth saying that the resurrection has already taken place, and they upset the faith of some.

19 Nevertheless, the firm foundation of God stands, having this seal, "The Lord knows those who are His," and, "Everyone who names the name of the Lord is to abstain from wickedness." **67**

20 Now in a large house there are not only gold and silver vessels,

Observation Worksheets—2 Timothy   163

but also vessels of wood and of earthenware, and some to honor and some to dishonor.

21 Therefore, if anyone cleanses himself from these things, he will be a vessel for honor, sanctified, useful to the Master, prepared for every good work.

22 Now flee from youthful lusts and pursue righteousness, faith,

(page 86)

remind (circle in blue)

gospel (and synonyms for the gospel: *these things* [verse 14], *word of truth* [verse 15], *the truth* [verse18]) (draw a red megaphone like this: and color it green.)

God (Father, Lord) (draw a purple triangle and color it yellow)

ashamed (turned away) (draw a brown arch over it like this: ⌒)

Don't forget to mark your pronouns!

All right! Now, let's ask the 5 W's and an H.

2 Timothy 2:14 WHAT is Paul's instruction to Timothy?

Remind them of these things

Turn to page 162 and draw a green box around this instruc-

Guided Instruction

64 Turn to page 162, reread 2 Timothy 2:14-21 aloud using your Observation Worksheet visual aid as students follow along and call out each new key word. Then mark them together as we noted on p. 13.

Remind (circle in blue)

Gospel (and synonyms for the Gospel: these things [verse 14], word of truth [verse 15], the truth [verse 18]) (draw a red megaphone and color it green)

God (Father, Lord) (draw a purple triangle and color it yellow)

Ashamed (turned away) (draw a brown arch over it)

Reread the selected verses and answer the questions.

2 Timothy 2:14 WHAT is Paul's instruction to Timothy? <u>Remind them of these things</u>

Turn to page 162 and draw a green box around this instruction.

Guided Instruction

To WHOM is Timothy to entrust these things? Faithful men

2 Timothy 2:14 WHAT does Paul tell Timothy to charge them? WHAT are they not to do? Wrangle about words

WHY? Useless; leads to the ruin of the hearers

2. Timothy 2:15 WHAT is Paul's instruction? Be diligent to present yourself approved to God.

65 Turn to page 162 and draw green boxes around these instructions (Teacher Guide page 93).

2 Timothy 2:15 WHAT are you to be like? A workman, not ashamed

WHY doesn't the workman have to be ashamed? Because he's accurately handling the word of truth

Lead a discussion about the text below this question.

(page 86)

Turn to page 162 and draw a green box around this instruction. WHO is the *them*? Do you know? Look back at 2 Timothy 2:2.

Timothy is to entrust these things to WHOM?

Faithful men

2 Timothy 2:14 WHAT does Paul tell Timothy to charge them? WHAT are they not to do?

Wrangle about words

WHY? Useless; leads to the ruin of the hearers

Handle God's Word Accurately   87

2 Timothy 2:15 WHAT is Paul's instruction?

Be diligent to present yourself approved to God.

To be diligent is to make an effort, to be careful in your work. Turn to page 162 and draw a green box around this instruction.

2 Timothy 2:15 WHAT are you to be like?

A workman, not ashamed

WHY doesn't the workman have to be ashamed?

Because he's accurately handling the word of truth

We have to be careful how we handle God's Word. God's Word is just that—it is God's Word. It is not to be changed or twisted or made to say what you want it to say. It is the truth! It shows us how to live. And only if you handle it that way will you be approved by God. The Greek word for *approved* is *dokimos*, which is pronounced like this: *dok-ee-mos*. *Dokimos* means to be put to the test and to pass the test.

Are you careful with God's Word? Do you study it so you make sure you know WHAT it says? Or do you just listen to WHAT others teach and believe WHAT they say? Write out WHAT you do.

(page 87)

By the way, you're studying it for yourself right now! Way to go—we are so proud of you!

2 Timothy 2:16 WHAT is Paul's instruction?

Avoid worldly and empty chatter.

WHY? **It will lead to further ungodliness.**

---

88   WEEK FOUR

Turn to page 162 and draw a green box around this instruction.

2 Timothy 2:17 WHAT do we see about this kind of talking? **Spreads like gangrene**

2 Timothy 2:17-18 WHO are these men who talk like this? **Men who have gone astray from the truth**

2 Timothy 2:18 WHAT are they saying that is not true?

That the resurrection has taken place

If what they are teaching is not true, are they false teachers? **Yes**

Are they accurately handling God's Word? **No**

2 Timothy 2:19 WHAT do we see about God's foundation? **It is firm. It stands.**

2 Timothy 2:19 WHAT is this seal?

The **Lord** **knows** those who are **His** , and, **everyone** who **names** the **name** of the **Lord** is to **abstain** from **wickedness** .

Awesome! God knows those who are really His! You may fool some people into thinking you are a believer but you can't fool God!

Guided Instruction

2 Timothy 2:16 WHAT is Paul's instruction? Avoid worldly and empty chatter.

WHY? It will lead to further ungodliness.

66 Draw a green box around this instruction (Teacher Guide page 93).

2 Timothy 2:17 WHAT do we see about this kind of talking? Spreads like gangrene

2 Timothy 2:17-18 WHO are these men who talk like this? Men who have gone astray from the truth

2 Timothy 2:18 WHAT are they saying that is *not* true? That the resurrection has taken place

IF what they are teaching is not true, are they false teachers? Yes

ARE they accurately handling God's Word? No

2 Timothy 2:19 WHAT do we see about God's foundation? It is firm. It stands.

2 Timothy 2:19 WHAT is this seal? The Lord knows those who are His, and, everyone who names the name of the Lord is to abstain from wickedness.

Guided Instruction

2 Timothy 2:19 WHAT is the instruction to the one who names the name of the Lord? Abstain from wickedness!

67 Turn to page 162 and draw a green box around this instruction (Teacher Guide page 93).

Discuss the following text and have students answer independently.

Look up and read 1 Corinthians 9:26-27 and answer the questions.

WHAT are we to do to our body?
Discipline it

WHY? So that we won't be disqualified

Practice saying the memory verse with a friend (Teacher Guide page 91).

Handle God's Word Accurately   89

2 Timothy 2:19 WHAT is the instruction to the one who names the name of the Lord?

Abstain from wickedness!

Turn to page 162 and draw a green box around this instruction.

All right! Way to go! Today as we looked at Paul's instructions to Timothy, we saw that Timothy was to remind faithful men about the gospel and to charge them not to wrangle, to argue with words that will hurt those who are listening. They were to be diligent, to be careful how they handled God's Word, to make sure they were teaching the truth, and to avoid worldly and empty chatter. Do you ever hear people who are always arguing about the Bible being untrue? That is worldly and empty chatter.

We also saw that God knows those who are really His! And if we are His, we are to abstain from wickedness! Remember, the things we believe and the things we do show whether we are true believers in Jesus Christ.

Are you doing that? Do you stay away from things you know are wrong? Name something wrong that you stay away from.

_____

Look up and read 1 Corinthians 9:26-27.

WHAT are we to do to our body?
Discipline it

WHY? **So that we won't be disqualified**

Isn't that cool? We are to discipline our body in such a way that we won't be disqualified. The word *disqualified* in this verse is *dokimos*, the same Greek word translated "approved" in 2 Timothy 2:15. We are to compete in such a way that when we are tested we will pass the test!

Tomorrow we will find out more about those who belong to

---

90   WEEK FOUR

God and those who don't. Don't forget to practice your memory verse as you head back to the gym for more fun!

(page 90)

DAY THREE
STICK IT!

68

Molly, Katie, Morgan, and Bethany sat in the stands as the boys got ready for their turn in the floor exercise. "How do you think the boys will do?" Morgan asked Molly. "They have been practicing really hard...I think they will do well."

"There goes Wes," Morgan said as Wes flipped across the mat.

The girls stood up and cheered as the boys finished. "Way to go, guys; you did great!" Coach Neighbors congratulated Wes on his bronze medal. "Way to go, buddy! That was some hard work! All you guys did well. Let's go meet the girls."

Let's head back to 2 Timothy 2. Pray and ask God to help you. Turn to page 162 and read 2 Timothy 2:20-21.

Let's ask the 5 W's and an H to solve the crossword puzzle on the next page.

(page 162)

69 ...mes the name of the Lord is to abstain from wickedness.

20 Now in a large house there are not only gold and silver vessels,

Observation Worksheets—2 Timothy 163

but also vessels of wood and of earthenware, and some to honor and some to dishonor.

21 Therefore, if anyone cleanses himself from these things, he will be a vessel for honor, sanctified, useful to the Master, prepared for every good work.

22 Now flee f........ .....thful lusts and pursue righteousness, faith,

Guided Instruction

DAY THREE

Ask God to fill your mind and heart with His message today.

68 Turn to page 90 and read "Stick it!"

69 Turn to page 162 and read 2 Timothy 2:20-21.

Guided Instruction

70 Answer the questions to complete the crossword puzzle on page 91.

2 Timothy 2:20 WHERE are these vessels? 1. (Down) In a <u>large</u> **2. (Across)** <u>house</u>

2 Timothy 2:20 WHAT do we see about these vessels?

Some are vessels to 3. (Across) Some are vessels to <u>honor</u> and some to **4. (Down)** <u>dishonor</u>

2 Timothy 2:21 HOW are we to be vessels of honor?

5. (Down) If anyone <u>cleanses</u> himself from these things

Look up 1 Corinthians 15:33

WHAT does bad company do?

6. (Across) <u>corrupts</u> good **7. (Across)** <u>morals</u>

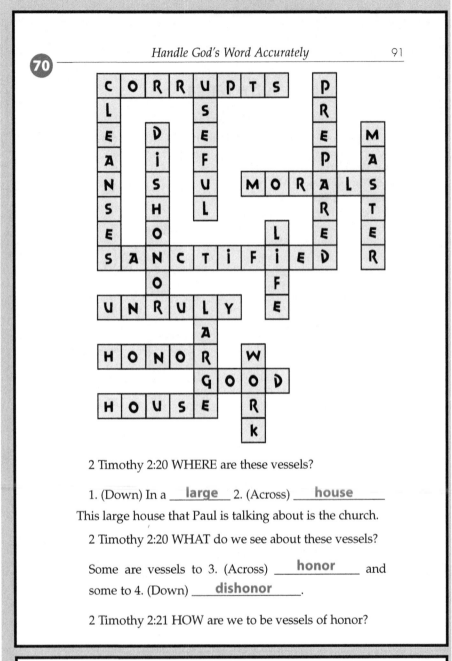

70   *Handle God's Word Accurately*   91

2 Timothy 2:20 WHERE are these vessels?

1. (Down) In a ___large___ 2. (Across) ___house___
This large house that Paul is talking about is the church.

2 Timothy 2:20 WHAT do we see about these vessels?

Some are vessels to 3. (Across) ___honor___ and some to 4. (Down) ___dishonor___.

2 Timothy 2:21 HOW are we to be vessels of honor?

92   WEEK FOUR

5. (Down) If anyone ___cleanses___ himself from these things

Look up and read 1 Corinthians 15:33 to see HOW we can cleanse ourselves and be vessels of honor.

1 Corinthians 15:33 WHAT does bad company do?

6. (Across) ___corrupts___ good 7. (Across) ___morals___

(page 92)

So to be vessels of honor, we need to cleanse ourselves by separating from vessels of dishonor. We need to be careful about the company we keep, whom we hang out with. Look up and read 2 Thessalonians 3:6.

2 Thessalonians 3:6 WHOM are we to keep away from?

Every brother who leads an 8. (Across) ___**unruly**___

9. (Down) ___**life**___

2 Timothy 2:21 If we are vessels of honor, WHAT will we be?

10. (Across) __**sanctified**__ , 11. (Down) ___**useful**___

to the 12. (Down) __**Master**__ , 13. (Down) __**prepared**__

for every 14. (Across) ___**good**___ 15. (Down)

___**work**___

Wow! Which do you want to be—a vessel of honor that is sanctified, set apart, and useful to God for every good work, or a vessel of dishonor?

_____

Which of these vessels represents believers?

_____

Guided Instruction

Look up the selected verses from 2 Thessalonians 3:6 and 2 Timothy 2:21 to complete the crossword puzzle.

2 Thessalonians 3:6 WHOM are we to keep away from?

Every brother who leads an **8. (Across)** unruly **9. (Down)** life

2 Timothy 2:21 If we are vessels of honor, WHAT will we be?

10. (Across) sanctified **11. (Down)** useful to the **12. (Down)** Master, **13. (Down)** prepared for every **14. (Across)** good **15. (Down)** work

Read and discuss the following text through page 93 and have students respond to the statements.

Practice saying the memory verse with a friend (Teacher Guide page 91).

Guided Instruction

Which of these vessels represents unbelievers?

_____

Today we have seen two different types of vessels in the church—those that are of gold and silver and are for honor, and those that are wood and earthenware for dishonor.

To be a vessel of honor that God can use, we have to cleanse ourselves from these things, these vessels of dishonor. Remember, bad company corrupts good morals. Second Corinthians 6:14 says, "Do not be bound together with unbelievers; for what partnership have righteousness and lawlessness, or what fellowship has light with darkness?"

In order to be used by God, we have to be set apart—different from the world we live in. Do you hang out with kids who care nothing about God? _____ Watch out!

WHAT kind of kids do you hang out with? Kids who love God and do what God says is right or kids who go in the opposite direction, who do what pleases them, and who participate in the things that God says are sin?

_____

WHAT are your best friends like? Put a checkmark next to the statements that apply to them.

- Your best friends obey their parents. _____

- Your best friends don't raise their voices and talk ugly to their parents. They respect their parents. _____

- Your best friends lie to their parents. _____

- Your best friends go to movies they shouldn't see. _____

- Your best friends use bad words. _____

Vessels of honor have to separate themselves from vessels of dishonor, from those who are walking in the opposite direction from God and who are living an ungodly lifestyle. We saw that we are to keep away from a brother who lives an unruly life. If we

are set apart and allowing God to work in our hearts and our lives, then we will be prepared to do whatever God asks us to do.

WHAT else can you learn about being a vessel of honor that God can use? You'll find out tomorrow as you continue to look at 2 Timothy 2. Here's a hint: Practice your memory verse.

DAY FOUR

SOMERSAULT INTO ACTION

(page 94)

71

"Hey, Max," Molly looked around. "Where's Sam?" Max turned around and looked for Sam.

"Uh-oh, we're in trouble now." Max moaned. "Let's spread out to look for him. You know how he loves to get into mischief. Sam, Sam, where are you, boy?" Max whistled as he called for Sam.

Coach Neighbors walked up to Max. "Hey, Max, don't worry about Sam. One of the coaches saw him wandering around and took him for a little special training. You know how bad he's wanted to get out on the exercise mat. Well, Coach Allen decided to give him a chance to do his own floor exercise. Why don't you and the team start your training on 2 Timothy."

Let's head back to 2 Timothy 2. Don't forget to talk to God.

Turn to page 163. Read 2 Timothy 2:22-26 and mark the key words listed below (and their synonyms).

gospel (the truth) (draw a red megaphone like this: ◁◖ and color it green)

God (Father, Lord) (draw a purple triangle and color it yellow)

Yesterday as we looked at the vessels in a large house (the church), we saw a contrast. We saw some vessels of honor and some vessels of dishonor. We saw that to be a vessel of honor we

---

(page 163)

...y good work.

72

22 Now flee from youthful lusts and pursue righteousness, faith, **73 74** love and peace, with those who call on the Lord from a pure heart.

23 But refuse foolish and ignorant speculations, knowing that they produce quarrels. **75**

24 The Lord's bond-servant must not be quarrelsome, but be kind to all, able to teach, patient when wronged,

25 with gentleness correcting those who are in opposition, if perhaps God may grant them repentance leading to the knowledge of the truth,

26 and they may come to their senses and escape from the snare of the devil, having been held captive by him to do his will.

Guided Instruction

DAY FOUR

Ask God to help you internalize His Word so that you will be a vessel of honor.

71 Turn to page 94 and read "Somersault into Action."

72 Turn to page 163 and read 2 Timothy 2:22-26 aloud using your Observation Worksheet visual aid as students follow along and call out each key word. Then mark them together as we noted on p. 13.

Gospel (the truth) (draw a red megaphone and color it green)

God (Father, Lord) (draw a purple triangle and color it yellow)

Guided Instruction

2 Timothy 2:22 WHAT is the first instruction? WHAT are you to do?

F l e e from youthful lusts.

73 Turn to page 163 and draw a green box around this instruction (Teacher Guide page 101).

Discuss the next question on page 95 and have students respond.

---

are to cleanse ourselves, and we learned that one way we can do that is to watch the company we keep. WHAT else can we do to be set apart and useful to the Master for every good work?

Two instructions in 2 Timothy 2:22 show us how to become vessels of honor. WHAT is the first instruction? WHAT are you to do?

F l e e from ___youthful___ ___lusts___.

Turn to page 163 and draw a green box around this instruction.

Wow! Have you ever turned on your computer and seen something you shouldn't see? When you are tempted, you are to flee, to run away from youthful lusts. Lusts are wrong desires and impulses that lead to sin. In order to be a vessel of honor, you need to get away from anything—a thought, an action, or even people—that will lead you to sin.

WHAT are you going to do the next time you are tempted to say a bad word, look at something on the Internet you know is wrong, or hang out with the wrong crowd? _____

WEEK FOUR
96

2 Timothy 2:22 WHAT are you to do after you flee? WHAT is the second instruction?

P u r s u e **righteousness** , **faith** , **love** , and **peace**

Turn to page 163 and draw a green box around this instruction.

HOW do you pursue righteousness? HOW do you know the right thing to do? WHAT do you need to do every day so you can know God and do what He says is right?

_____.

HOW do you pursue faith? Faith is taking God at His Word. Faith is believing Him and showing it by the way you act. Do you listen and pay attention to His Word?_____

WHAT do you do that shows you believe God?

_____

Have you accepted Jesus Christ as your Savior? Have you trusted God with your life? _____

_____

HOW can you pursue love? Look up and read Mark 12:30-31.

Mark 12:30 WHAT are you to do?
Love the Lord with all your heart, with all your soul, with all your mind, and all your stength.

Mark 12:31 WHOM else are you to love?

Your neighbor

Guided Instruction

Read the selected scripture to answer the questions on pages 96-99.

2 Timothy 2:22 WHAT are you to do after you flee? WHAT is the second instruction? P u r s u e righteousness, faith, love, and peace.

74 Turn to page 163 and draw a green box around this instruction (Teacher Guide page 101).

Lead a discussion and have students answer the next four questions.

HOW can you pursue love? Look and read Mark 12:30-31.

Mark 12:30 WHAT are you to do? Love the Lord with all your heart, with all your soul, with all your mind, and all your stength.

Mark 12:31 WHOM else are you to love? Your neighbor

Guided Instruction

Independently answer the next question on page 97.

2 Timothy 2:24 WHAT must the Lord's bond-servant not be?
Q u a r r e l s o m e

Independently answer the next two questions.

2 Timothy 2:22 WHOM are we to pursue these things with? Those who call on the Lord with a pure heart

Lead a discussion before responding to the next question.

Handle God's Word Accurately   97

Wow! We are to love others and even put them before ourselves. And that doesn't just mean the people we like. We are to love everyone—even our enemies (Matthew 5:44).

Write out a way you are going to love your neighbor.

_____

HOW will you pursue peace? Look at 2 Timothy 2:24. WHAT must the Lord's bond-servant not be?

Q u a r r e l s o m e

One way you can pursue peace is to try to get along with others.

WHOM do you fuss and argue with—your parents, your brothers or sisters, kids at school, your teacher...?

_____

WHAT can you do to get along with others?

_____

Now, look back at 2 Timothy 2:22. WHOM are we to pursue these things with?

Those who **call on the Lord with a pure heart**

_____

Once again you see the importance of hanging out with the right kids. You need to be friends with kids who pursue God, kids who have a pure heart.

WHOM do you hang out with—kids who follow God,

or kids who are cool and popular? _____

_____

98   WEEK FOUR

If you don't have a friend who follows God, ask God to help you find one whom you can get to know and hang out with.

2 Timothy 2:23 WHAT is Paul's instruction?

Refuse foolish and ignorant speculation.

WHY? WHAT do they produce? **Quarrels**

Turn to page 163 and draw a green box around this instruction.

2 Timothy 2:24-25 WHAT do we learn about the Lord's bond-servant?

Must not be quarrelsome, but be kind to all, able to teach, patient when wronged, with gentleness correcting those in opposition

Do you know what a bond-servant is? A bond-servant is a person who has chosen to be a slave after he has been offered his freedom. To be a bond-servant is to willingly become a slave for life. To be God's bond-servant is to totally surrender your life to serve God and Jesus.

Have you considered telling the Lord you want to be His bond-servant? Have you surrendered your life and your way for God's way? _____

Do you have the qualities of a bond-servant listed in 2 Timothy 2:24-25? Write out the qualities that you see in your life.

_____

_____

WHAT qualities do you need to ask God to help you work on?

_____

Guided Instruction

2 Timothy 2:23 WHAT is Paul's instruction? Refuse foolish and ignorant speculation.

WHY? WHAT do they produce?
Quarrels

75 Turn to page 163 and draw a green box around this instruction (Teacher Guide page 101).

2 Timothy 2:24-25 WHAT do we learn about the Lord's bond-servant? Must not be quarrelsome, but be kind to all, able to teach, patient when wronged, with gentleness correcting those in opposition

Lead a discussion about the meaning of the word *bond-servant*. Consider the personal question and respond.

2 Timothy 2:24-25 Write out the qualities of a bond-servant that you see in your life.

WHAT qualities do you need to ask God to help you work on?

Guided Instruction

2 Timothy 2:25 WHY are we to have these qualities in our lives? WHAT are we to do with gentleness? Correct those in opposition.

Discuss the text about those in opposition.

2 Timothy 2:25 WHAT may God grant these vessels of dishonor? Repentance leading to knowledge of the truth

2 Timothy 2:26 WHOM are they held captive to? The devil

2 Timothy 2:26 WHAT may happen to them? They may come to their senses and escape from the snare of the devil.

Practice saying the memory verse (Teacher Guide page 91).

Handle God's Word Accurately   99

2 Timothy 2:25 WHY are we to have these qualities in our lives? WHAT are we to do with gentleness?

Correct those in opposition.

Did you get it? We are not to quarrel with those who are opposing God. We are to be kind and gentle with them when we correct what they are doing wrong. We are to be able to teach them, to show them what they are doing or believing is wrong. And we are also to be patient if they lash out or hurt us.

We are to show people the truth, but we are to do it with the character of Jesus, not getting mad and responding in anger. We are to show them that we are different and that we belong to Jesus by the way we act and treat them. And WHAT may happen?

2 Timothy 2:25 WHAT may God grant these vessels of dishonor?

Repentance leading to knowledge of the truth

2 Timothy 2:26 WHOM are they held captive by?

The devil

2 Timothy 2:26 WHAT may happen to them?

They may come to their senses and escape from the snare of the devil.

Wow! When you act like Jesus by correcting others with gentleness and showing them the truth, God may allow them to come to their senses so that they repent and turn to the truth. Isn't that awesome! What a way for God to use you!

Now, don't forget to practice your memory verse.

100   WEEK FOUR

DAY FIVE

76 ## SHOWTIME!

Are you ready to see Sam in action? Look, here he comes! Look at those ribbons he is carrying in his mouth. He is going to do some rhythmic gymnastics. WOW! Did you see that? Sam did a flip! There he goes, jumping through a ring this time. Amazing! Will Sam get a medal? The crowd is going crazy. Uh-oh, there he goes. He sees Max. All right! Way to go, Sam!

Wasn't that fun watching Sam? He was feeling a little left out, but not anymore. Now he has his own medal. Give Sam a doggie treat and let's head back to 2 Timothy 2.

Have you noticed that Paul shows Timothy how to distinguish between the believers and the unbelievers? Today we want to look back at 2 Timothy 2:14-26 and find the characteristics that describe believers and unbelievers, just as we did on day one for 2 Timothy 2:1-13.

Handle God's Word Accurately   101

Don't forget to pray and ask God to help you see what describes a true believer and what describes an unbeliever.

Turn to page 162 and read 2 Timothy 2:14-26. As you read each verse, ask yourself WHOM this describes?

Guided Instruction

DAY FIVE

Ask God to lead you to clear understanding of this lesson.

76 Turn to page 100 and read "Showtime!"

Guided Instruction

77 Turn to page 162 and reread 2 Timothy 2:14-26 and answer the question about WHOM this describes.

(page 162)

77 14 Remind them of these things, and solemnly charge them in the presence of God not to wrangle about words, which is useless and leads to the ruin of the hearers.

15 Be diligent to present yourself approved to God as a workman who does not need to be ashamed, accurately handling the word of truth.

16 But avoid worldly and empty chatter, for it will lead to further ungodliness,

17 and their talk will spread like gangrene. Among them are Hymenaeus and Philetus,

18 men who have gone astray from the truth saying that the resurrection has already taken place, and they upset the faith of some.

19 Nevertheless, the firm foundation of God stands, having this seal, "The Lord knows those who are His," and, "Everyone who names the name of the Lord is to abstain from wickedness."

20 Now in a large house there are not only gold and silver vessels,

Observation Worksheets—2 Timothy   163

but also vessels of wood and of earthenware, and some to honor and some to dishonor.

21 Therefore, if anyone cleanses himself from these things, he will be a vessel for honor, sanctified, useful to the Master, prepared for every good work.

22 Now flee from youthful lusts and pursue righteousness, faith, love and peace, with those who call on the Lord from a pure heart.

23 But refuse foolish and ignorant speculations, knowing that they produce quarrels.

24 The Lord's bond-servant must not be quarrelsome, but be kind to all, able to teach, patient when wronged,

25 with gentleness correcting those who are in opposition, if perhaps God may grant them repentance leading to the knowledge of the truth,

26 and they may come to their senses and escape from the snare of the devil, having been held captive by him to do his will.

(page 101)

2 Timothy 2:14 WHO is the *them* in this verse? Remember, we saw that the *them* were the faithful men in 2 Timothy 2:2. So WHO are the faithful men—believers or unbelievers?

__Believers__

On the following chart, under Characteristics of a Believer, write what this verse tells us about a believer. Then fill in the rest of the chart, writing the characteristics from each verse that describe a believer.

78

Characteristics of a Believer

2 Timothy 2:14 A believer is not to __wrangle__ about __words__.

2 Timothy 2:15 Is d __i l i g e n t__. __Presents__ himself to God as a __workman__ who does not need to be __ashamed__, __accurately__ handling the __word__ of __truth__.

2 Timothy 2:16 Avoids __worldly__ and __empty chatter__.

2 Timothy 2:19 Abstains from __wickedness__.

2 Timothy 2:20 A vessel of __honor__.

2 Timothy 2:21 __Cleanses__ himself. He is s __a n c t i f i e d__, __useful__ to the

---

102 WEEK FOUR

__Master__, __prepared__ for every __good work__.

2 Timothy 2:22 __Flees__ from youthful __lusts__ and pursues __righteousness__, __faith__, __love__, and __peace__, with those who call on the Lord from a __pure__ heart.

2 Timothy 2:23 Refuses __foolish__ and __ignorant__ speculations.

2 Timothy 2:24 The Lord's __bond__ - __servant__, not __quarrelsome__, __kind__ to all, able to __teach__, __patient__ when wronged.

Guided Instruction

2 Timothy 2:14 WHO is the *them* in this verse? WHO are the *faithful men*—believers or unbelievers? Believers

78 Complete the chart about the characteristic of the believer.

Characteristics of a Believer

2 Timothy 2:14 A believer is not to wrangle about words.

2 Timothy 2:15 Is d i l i g e n t. Presents himself to God as a workman who does not need to be ashamed, accurately handling the word of truth

2 Timothy 2:16 Avoids worldly and empty chatter

2 Timothy 2:19 Abstains from wickedness

2 Timothy 2:20 A vessel of honor

2 Timothy 2:21 Cleanses himself. He is s a n c t i f i e d, useful to the Master, prepared for every good work.

2 Timothy 2:22 Flees from youthful lusts and pursues righteousness, faith, love, and peace, with those who call on the Lord from a pure heart

2 Timothy 2:23 Refuses foolish and ignorant speculations

2 Timothy 2:24 The Lord's bond-servant, not quarrelsome, kind to all, able to teach, patient when wronged

Guided Instruction

2 Timothy 2:25 Corrects with <u>gentleness</u> those who are in <u>opposition</u>

79 List characteristics of the unbeliever.

Characteristics of an Unbeliever

2 Timothy 2:17 Their <u>talk</u> spreads like <u>gangrene</u>.

2 Timothy 2:18 They have gone astray from the <u>truth</u> and upset the <u>faith</u> of some.

2 Timothy 2:20 Vessels of <u>dishonor</u>

2 Timothy 2:25 In o <u>p p o s i t i o n</u> to God.

2 Timothy 2:26 In the snare of the <u>devil</u>, held <u>captive</u> by him to do his <u>will</u>

Practice the memory verse with a friend.

Thank God for the privilege of studying His Word.

If you are a Sunday School teacher this is a great time to review the whole week by playing a game like *The Matching Game* on page 164 or the *5W and H Game* on page 166. This is also a great way for classroom teachers and homeschool families to review with students what they learned this week.

If you are a classroom teacher you may want to give your students a quiz on their memory verse. There is also a quiz on Week Four on page 158 to check memory and understanding.

Memory Verse

"Now flee from youthful lusts and pursue righteousness, faith, love and peace, with those who call on the Lord with a pure heart."
2 Timothy 2:22

(page 102)

2 Timothy 2:25 Corrects with ____gentleness____ those who are in ___opposition___.

Now look back at these same verses and list any characteristics in the chart below that describe an unbeliever.

79

Characteristics of an Unbeliever

2 Timothy 2:17 Their _____talk_____ spreads like _gangrene_.

2 Timothy 2:18 They have gone astray from the ___truth___ and upset the ___faith___ of some.

2 Timothy 2:20 Vessels of ___dishonor___.

2 Timothy 2:25 In o _p o s i t i o n_ to God.

Handle God's Word Accurately   103

2 Timothy 2:26 In the snare of the ___devil___, held ___captive___ by him to do his ___will___.

Wow, which characteristics do you have?

_____

_____

Think about what you have learned. Now say your memory verse to a grown-up to remind you of what you are to do to be a vessel of honor! We are so proud of you!

5

CONTINUE IN THE THINGS YOU HAVE LEARNED

80

2 TIMOTHY 3

Are you ready for another exciting week in our summer games?

Last week as we looked at Paul's instructions to Timothy, we saw that Timothy was to remind faithful men about the gospel and to charge them to not wrangle about words. They were to be diligent and to accurately handle God's Word, making sure they were teaching the truth!

We also saw that the church includes vessels of honor that are set apart and useful to God, and vessels of dishonor. And that as the Lord's bond-servants, we are to correct those who are in opposition so that God may lead them to repent and turn to the truth! What a way to be a champion for God!

WHAT we will learn this week? Let's head to the archery field and find out.

DAY ONE

BRACING THE BOW

"Okay, guys, brace the bow," Coach Neighbors told Team USA

105

Guided Instruction

WEEK 5

DAY ONE

Ask God to keep you focused on His message today.

80 Turn to page 105 and read "2 Timothy 3" and "Bracing the Bow."

Guided Instruction

81 Turn to page 163 and read 2 Timothy 3 aloud using your Observation Worksheet visual aid as students follow along and call out each key word. Then mark them together as we noted on p. 13.

Reread this chapter and mark the key words.

God (Father) (draw a purple triangle and color it yellow)

Suffering (persecutions, persecuted) (draw a red squiggly line)

Christ Jesus (draw a purple cross and color it yellow)

words of encouragement (draw a pink cloud around each one) (verses 10, 11, and 15)

instructions (draw a green box around each one) (verses 1, 5, and 14)

WHERE (double underline words that denote place)

WHEN (draw a green clock over words that denote time)

---

106   WEEK FIVE

as they got out their bows on the field. "Now, stand, nock (set the arrow in the bowstring), and draw. Looking good. Release and follow through. All right, guys, that was great! Walk over to your target and see how you did. That was a great archery practice.

"Now pull out your books, and let's get some Bible training in. Bethany, why don't you pray for us."

Let's turn to page 163. Read 2 Timothy 3 and mark the key words listed below (and their synonyms).

God (Father) (draw a purple triangle and color it yellow)

suffering (persecutions, persecuted) (draw a red squiggly line like this: *///*)

Christ Jesus (draw a purple cross and color it yellow)

Look in verses 10, 11, and 15 for any exhortations that Paul gives Timothy and draw a pink cloud around the words of encouragement.

Verses 1, 5, and 14 contain three instructions to Timothy. Draw a green box around each instruction.

Don't forget to mark anything that tells you WHERE by double underlining the WHERE in green. Mark anything that tells you WHEN by drawing a green clock 🕐 or green circle like this: ◯ .

(page 163)

Guided Instruction

 Chapter 3

1 But realize this, that in the last days difficult times will come.

2 For men will be lovers of self, lovers of money, boastful, arrogant, revilers, disobedient to parents, ungrateful, unholy,

3 unloving, irreconcilable, malicious gossips, without self-control, brutal, haters of good,

4 treacherous, reckless, conceited, lovers of pleasure rather than lovers of God,

5 holding to a form of godliness, although they have denied its power; avoid such men as these.

6 For among them are those who enter into households and captivate weak women weighed down with sins, led on by various impulses,

164 *Observation Worksheets*

7 always learning and never able to come to the knowledge of the truth.

8 Just as Jannes and Jambres opposed Moses, so these men also oppose the truth, men of depraved mind, rejected in regard to the faith.

9 But they will not make further progress; for their folly will be obvious to all, just as Jannes's and Jambres's folly was also.

10 Now you followed my teaching, conduct, purpose, faith, patience, love, perseverance,

11 persecutions, and sufferings, such as happened to me at Antioch, at Iconium and at Lystra; what persecutions I endured, and out of them all the Lord rescued me!

12 Indeed, all who desire to live godly in Christ Jesus will be persecuted.

13 But evil men and impostors will proceed from bad to worse, deceiving and being deceived.

14 You, however, continue in the things you have learned and become convinced of, knowing from whom you have learned them,

15 and that from childhood you have known the sacred writings which are able to give you the wisdom that leads to salvation through faith which is in Christ Jesus.

16 All Scripture is inspired by God and profitable for teaching, for reproof, for correction, for training in righteousness;

17 so that the man of God may be adequate, equipped for every good work.

Guided Instruction

82 Solve the memory verse on page 107.

You, however, (1) <u>continue</u> in the (2) <u>things</u> you have (3) <u>learned</u> and become (4) <u>convinced</u> of, knowing from (5) <u>whom</u> you have (6) <u>learned</u> (7) <u>them</u>.

          2 Timothy 3:<u>15</u>

Copy the memory verse to an index card and practice saying it three times, three times each day.

(page 106)

Fantastic! Let's discover our memory verse. Look at the arrows in the target on the next page. Each arrow has a number on the feather. Look at the number and find the matching blank

---

Continue in the Things You Have Learned   107

below. Write the word written on each arrow on the correct blank to solve this week's verse. Then turn to 2 Timothy 3 and find the reference for this verse.

82

You, however, <u>**continue**</u> in the <u>**things**</u> you have
            1   2

<u>**learned**</u> and become <u>**convinced**</u> of,
  3   4

knowing from <u>**whom**</u> you have <u>**learned**</u>
           5   6

<u>**them**</u>.   2 Timothy 3: <u>15</u>
  7

Now write it out and practice saying it three times in a row today. Stand, nock, draw, release, and follow through! Way to hit the target!

108   WEEK FIVE

DAY TWO

(83) ## AIMING FOR THE TARGET

"Max, you're up." Coach Neighbors stood beside Max, giving him his last-minute instructions. "Remember, when your drawing hand reaches your anchor point, hold it tight against your face for a few seconds to steady your aim. Keep your eyes on the bull's-eye.

"Next, tighten your back and shoulder muscles, open the fingers of your drawing hand, and release."

"You can do it, Max," cheered the rest of Team USA while Sam barked his agreement.

All right! Did you see that? Max got a 5, a 7, an 8, another 8, and a bull's-eye. Way to go, Max! Team USA is on its way to another medal!

Now, let's head back to our Bible training and give our best to God. Don't forget to pray. Turn to page 163 and read 2 Timothy 3:1-5.

(page 163)

(84) **Chapter 3**

1 But realize this, that in the last days difficult times will come.

2 For men will be lovers of self, lovers of money, boastful, arrogant, revilers, disobedient to parents, ungrateful, unholy,

3 unloving, irreconcilable, malicious gossips, without self-control, brutal, haters of good,

4 treacherous, reckless, conceited, lovers of pleasure rather than lovers of God,

5 holding to a form of godliness, although they have denied its power; avoid such men as these.

6 For ~~among them are those who enter into households~~ and

Let's ask the 5 W's and an H.   (page 108)

2 Timothy 3:1 WHAT is Paul's instruction?

R e a l i z e t h i s

Did you remember to put a green box around this instruction?

2 Timothy 3:1 WHEN is this going to happen?

In the last days

Did you know that we are living in the last days right now? The last days started when Jesus began His ministry on earth and will end when He comes back again the second time. We are living in the last days!

Guided Instruction

DAY TWO

Tell God how grateful you are to have His Word. Ask him to guide you to clear understanding.

(83) Turn to page 108 and read "Aiming for the Target."

(84) Turn to page 163 and reread 2 Timothy 3:1-5 to answer the questions.

2 Timothy 3:1 WHAT is Paul's instruction? R e a l i z e t h i s

2 Timothy 3:1 WHEN is this going to happen? In the last days (Discuss this phrase)

Guided Instruction

2 Timothy 3:1 WHAT do we need to realize? WHAT is going to happen in the last days? <u>Difficult times will come.</u>

Discuss the Greek word for "men" in verse 2: *anthropos.*

2 Timothy 3:2-5 HOW are these men described? List their characteristics.

<u>Lovers of self and money, boastful, arrogant, revilers, disobedient to parents, ungrateful, unholy, unloving, irreconcilable, malicious gossips, no self-control, brutal, haters of good, treacherous, reckless, conceited, lovers of pleasure rather than God, holding a form of godliness though they have denied its power.</u>

Continue in the Things You Have Learned   109

2 Timothy 3:1 WHAT do we need to realize? WHAT is going to happen in the last days?
<u>Difficult times will come.</u>

That means things will continue to get worse and worse and worse, and yet the world will think things will get better and better.

Did you know that the New Testament, where the book of 2 Timothy is found, was originally written in Koine Greek? The Greek word for the word *men* in verse 2 is *anthrôpos.* It is pronounced like this: *anth-ro-pos.* This word means a human being, people, or mankind. So when you read verse 2, the word for *men* actually refers to all people, not just men.

2 Timothy 3:2-5 HOW are these men (people) described?

List the characteristics of these men. <u>**Lovers of self and money, boastful, arrogant, revilers, disobedient to parents, ungrateful, unholy, unloving, irreconcilable, malicious gossips, no self-control, brutal, haters of good, treacherous, reckless, conceited, lovers of pleasure rather than God, holding a form of godliness though they have denied its power.**</u>

110   WEEK FIVE

Are these characteristics of believers or unbelievers?
Unbelievers

Let's look at a few of these characteristics and think about what they mean.

WHAT does it mean to be a lover of self?

Do you remember what we saw last week in Mark 12:30-31 as we looked at pursuing love? We saw that we are to love God with all our heart, with all our soul, with all our mind, and with all our strength. And we are to love others as ourselves. A lover of self puts the focus on himself. It's all about *me*, not loving God or our neighbors. Are you a lover of self?

Do you love yourself more than others? __ Yes __ No

Do you have to be first and have your way? __ Yes __ No

Do you put yourself ahead of others? __ Yes __ No

Look up and read Philippians 2:3-8.

Philippians 2:3 HOW are we to regard others?
As more important than ourselves

Philippians 2:6 WHO was Jesus? Jesus was G **o d**!

Philippians 2:7 WHAT did Jesus do?

He ____**emptied**____ Himself, taking on the form of a ____**bond**____-____**servant**____ .

Philippians 2:8 WHAT else did He do?

He __**humbled**__ Himself by becoming **obedient** to the point of death.

Guided Instruction

Are these characteristics of believers or unbelievers? Unbelievers

Lead students through application by discussing the personal questions on pages 110-113.

Look up and read the selected scripture to answer the questions.

Philippians 2:3 HOW are we to regard others? As more important than ourselves

Philippians 2:6 WHO was Jesus? Jesus was G o d!

Philippians 2:7 WHAT did Jesus do? He emptied Himself, taking on the form of a bond-servant.

Philippians 2:8 WHAT else did He do? He humbled Himself by becoming obedient to the point of death.

Discuss the text and application questions on page 111.

Guided Instruction

Look up and read Ephesians 6:1-3 to answer the questions.

Ephesians 6:1-2 WHAT are children to do? <u>Obey and honor parents</u>

Ephesians 6:3 WHAT is the promise if you obey and honor your parents? <u>It will be well with you and you'll live long on the earth.</u>

We are to be like Jesus. Even though Jesus was God, He took on the form of a bond-servant, became a man, obeyed God, and gave up His life for us! *Amazing!* We are to humble ourselves by putting others first. We are not to love ourselves more than others. We are to give ourselves for others just as Jesus gave Himself for us!

Let's look at some other characteristics.

HOW important is money to you?

Matthew 6:24 tells us that we cannot serve two masters. We cannot serve God and wealth. HOW about you?

Do you covet (long with envy for) everything your friends have? _____ Yes _____ No

Are you greedy? Do you want more and more? Do you have to have the newest and the latest things? _____ Yes _____ No

Are you boastful?

Do you brag about how great you are or the things that you have, or do you realize that everything that you are and that you have comes from God? Write out what you do.

Are you disobedient to your parents?

Look up and read Ephesians 6:1-3.

Ephesians 6:1-2 WHAT are children to do?

<u>Obey and honor parents</u>

Ephesians 6:3 WHAT is the promise if you obey and honor your parents? <u>It will be well with you and you'll live long on the earth.</u>

112   WEEK FIVE

Are you ungrateful?

Do you bug your parents to buy things? Are you unsatisfied with the things that you have? ___ Yes ___ No

Are you thankful for the people who love you and the things God has blessed you with? ___ Yes ___ No

Look up and read 1 Thessalonians 5:18.

WHAT is God's will for you?

To give thanks in everything

Let's look at one more of these characteristics.

Do you hold to a form of godliness?

People who hold to a form of godliness are people who pretend to be Christians, but they are not really believers. They do religious things and act like Christians on the outside, but there isn't a change on the inside. They have not turned their lives over to Jesus. So HOW about you? Do you go to church and say all the right things but then do what you want to do instead of what pleases God? For example…

Do you lie to your parents? ___ Yes ___ No

Do you make fun of other kids? ___ Yes ___ No

Do you look at bad stuff on the Internet? ___ Yes ___ No

Wow! Do you see any of these descriptions in your life? If you do see any of these things in your life, WHAT do you do? Look up and read 1 John 1:9.

WHAT are we to do?

Confess our sins

WHAT will God do?

Forgive them and cleanse us

Guided Instruction

Look up and read 1 Thessalonians 5:18.

WHAT is God's will for you? To give thanks in everything

Look up and read 1 John 1:9 to answer the questions:

WHAT are we to do? Confess our sins

WHAT will God do? Forgive them and cleanse us

Guided Instruction

Look up and read 2 Timothy 3:5 to answer the questions:

WHAT was Paul's instruction? <u>There are people who hold to godliness but deny its power.</u>

WHAT are we to do about the people we just described? <u>Avoid them</u>

Isn't that awesome? God loves you so much that He forgives you when you fail. But don't think these things don't matter. They do. It's easy to act like everybody else. People who are vessels of dishonor want us to act just like them. But we are to act like Jesus, not like everybody else. Ask God for His help so the world can see Jesus living in you!

And if you see that you are only pretending to be a Christian, tell a grown-up that you really want to know Jesus and have a relationship with Him, and he or she will help you give your life to Jesus.

> Look back at 2 Timothy 3:5 WHAT was Paul's instruction?
>
> **There are people who hold to godliness but deny its power.**
>
> WHAT are we to do about the people we just described?
>
> **Avoid them**

Remember what we learned. Bad company corrupts good morals. To be vessels of honor that God can use, we need to stay away from people like these!

All right! You have hit the target again! Don't forget to practice your memory verse!

Guided Instruction

(page 113)

DAY THREE
HOLD AND RELEASE

86 Way to go! That was an awesome shot. What a steady arm and quick release. Team USA is so excited about those two bull's-eyes. You helped Team USA bring home another gold medal!

All right! Let's head back to 2 Timothy 3. Turn to page 163 and read 2 Timothy 3:6-9. Let's ask the 5 W's and an H to solve the crossword puzzle on the next page.

(page 163)

power; avoid such men as these.

87 6 For among them are those who enter into households and captivate weak women weighed down with sins, led on by various impulses,

164 *Observation Worksheets*

7 always learning and never able to come to the knowledge of the truth.

8 Just as Jannes and Jambres opposed Moses, so these men also oppose the truth, men of depraved mind, rejected in regard to the faith.

9 But they will not make further progress; for their folly will be obvious to all, just as Jannes's and Jambres's folly was also.

10 Now you followed my teaching, conduct, purpose, faith,

DAY THREE

Ask God for guidance as you study this lesson.

86 Turn to page 113 and read "Hold and Release."

87 Turn to page 163 and reread 2 Timothy 3:6-9 to answer the questions and complete the crossword puzzle on page 114.

Guided Instruction

2 Timothy 4:6 WHAT do we see about these men?

1. (Down) They <u>captivate</u> **2. (Across)** <u>weak</u> women.

2 Timothy 3:6 WHAT do you learn about these weak women?

They are weighed down with **3. (Across)** <u>sins</u> and led on by various **4. (Across)** <u>impulses</u>.

2 Timothy 3:7 WHAT do we learn about these men?

They are always **5. (Across)** <u>learning</u> and never able to come to the knowledge of the **6. (Down)** <u>truth</u>.

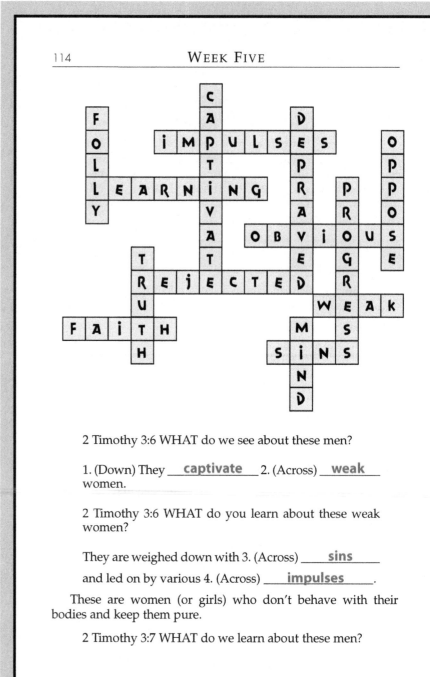

2 Timothy 3:6 WHAT do we see about these men?

1. (Down) They ___captivate___ 2. (Across) ___weak___ women.

2 Timothy 3:6 WHAT do you learn about these weak women?

They are weighed down with 3. (Across) ___sins___

and led on by various 4. (Across) ___impulses___.

These are women (or girls) who don't behave with their bodies and keep them pure.

2 Timothy 3:7 WHAT do we learn about these men?

They are always 5. (Across) ___learning___ and never able to come to the knowledge of the 6. (Down) ___truth___.

(page 115)

2 Timothy 3:8 WHAT do these men do?

7. (Down) They _____ **oppose** _____ the truth.

2 Timothy 3:8 WHAT are these men like?

They are men of 8. (Down) ____ **depraved** ____ 9. (Down) ____ **mind** ____, 10. (Across) ____ **rejected** ____ in regard to the 11. (Across) _____ **faith** _____.

2 Timothy 3:9 WHAT do we see about these men?

They will not make further 12. (Down) ___ **progress** ___; for their 13. (Down) _____ **folly** _____ will be 14. (Across) _____ **obvious** _____ to all.

Are you going to listen to false teachers, those who oppose truth?

2 Timothy 3:5 WHAT does Paul tell you to do?

_____ **Avoid** _____ such _____ **men** _____ as these.

Great work! We are to stay away from these false teachers. And we see that even though these men are opposing truth, they will not make further progress. Their false teaching will be exposed!

Hit the target one more time by practicing your memory verse!

Guided Instruction

2 Timothy 3:8 WHAT do these men do?

7. (Down) They <u>oppose</u> the truth.

2 Timothy 3:8 WHAT are these men like?

They are men of **8. (Down)** <u>depraved</u> **9. (Down)** <u>mind</u>, **10. (Across)** <u>rejected</u> in regard to the **11. (Across)** <u>faith</u>.

2 Timothy 3:9 WHAT do we see about these men?

They will not make further **12. (Down)** <u>progress</u> for their **13. (Down)** <u>folly</u> will be **14. (Across)** <u>obvious</u> to all.

2 Timothy 3:5 WHAT does Paul tell you to do? <u>Avoid</u> such <u>men</u> as these.

Practice saying the memory verse three times (Teacher Guide page 114).

Guided Instruction

DAY FOUR

Ask God to give you perseverance to remember His lesson today.

88 Turn to page 116 and read "Racing Uphill."

89 Turn to page 164 and reread 2 Timothy 3:10-13 to answer the questions.

2 Timothy 3:10-11 WHAT did Timothy do? Followed Paul's teaching, conduct, faith, patience, love and perseverance, persecutions and sufferings

2 Timothy 3:11 WHAT happened to Paul at Antioch, Iconium, and Lystra? He was persecuted and suffered.

Find and read 2 Corinthians 11:24-27.

HOW was Paul persecuted? He received thirty-nine lashes from the Jews five times.

He was beaten with rods three times.

He was stoned once.

He was shipwrecked three times.

---

116   WEEK FIVE

88

DAY FOUR
RACING UPHILL

That was a great archery competition! Our next event is biking.

Put on those bike helmets and fill up those water bottles. Then head to 2 Timothy 3 and prepare yourself for the race ahead. Don't forget to ask God for His help.

Turn to page 164 and read 2 Timothy 3:10-13. Ask the 5 W's and an H.

(page 164)

89

10 Now you followed my teaching, conduct, purpose, faith, patience, love, perseverance,

11 persecutions, and sufferings, such as happened to me at Antioch, at Iconium and at Lystra; what persecutions I endured, and out of them all the Lord rescued me!

12 Indeed, all who desire to live godly in Christ Jesus will be persecuted.

13 But evil men and impostors will proceed from bad to worse, deceiving and being deceived.

14 You, however, continue in the things you have learned and

(page 116)

2 Timothy 3:10-11 WHAT did Timothy do?
Followed Paul's teaching, conduct, faith, patience, love and perseverance, persecutions and sufferings

WHAT is Paul doing in these two verses? Paul is encouraging Timothy. Paul reminds Timothy of how Timothy has followed Paul's example. Did you put a pink cloud around this encouragement on your Observation Worksheet?

2 Timothy 3:11 WHAT happened to Paul at Antioch, Iconium, and Lystra? He was persecuted and suffered.

Look up and read 2 Corinthians 11:24-27. HOW was Paul persecuted?

He received thirty - nine lashes from the Jews five times.

He was beaten with rods three times.

He was stoned once.

He was shipwrecked three times.

He spent a ___night___ and a ___day___ in the ___deep___.

He has been in danger from ___rivers___, ___robbers___, his ___countrymen___ from the ___Gentiles___, in the ___city___, in the ___wilderness___, on the ___sea___, and among ___false___ ___brethren___.

He has been in ___labor___ and ___hardship___, through many ___sleepless___ ___nights___, in ___hunger___ and ___thirst___, often without ___food___, and in ___cold___ and exposure.

Draw a picture of one of Paul's persecutions in the box below

90

Go back to 2 Timothy 3:11 WHAT do we see about Paul?

Guided Instruction

He spent a <u>night</u> and a <u>day</u> in the <u>deep</u>.

He has been in danger from <u>rivers</u>, <u>robbers</u>, his <u>countrymen</u>, from the <u>Gentiles</u>, in the <u>city</u>, in the <u>wilderness</u>, on the <u>sea</u>, and among <u>false</u> <u>brethren</u>.

He has been in <u>labor</u> and <u>hardship</u> through many <u>sleepless</u> <u>nights</u>, in <u>hunger</u> and <u>thirst</u>, often without <u>food</u>, and in <u>cold</u> and exposure.

90 Draw a picture of one of Paul's persecutions in the box on page 117.

Guided Instruction

2 Timothy 3:11 WHAT do we see about Paul? He e n d u r e d!

2 Timothy 3:11 WHAT did the Lord do?
Rescued him

2 Timothy 3:12 WHAT will happen to those who desire to live godly in Christ Jesus? They will be persecuted.

2 Timothy 3:13 WHAT do you learn about evil men and imposters? They go from bad to worse, deceiving and being deceived.

Practicing saying the memory verse three times with a friend (Teacher Guide page 114).

---

118   WEEK FIVE

He e n d u r e d!

2 Timothy 3:11 WHAT did the Lord do?

Rescued him

Wow! WHAT an *awesome* God!

2 Timothy 3:12 WHAT will happen to those who desire to live godly in Christ Jesus?

They will be persecuted.

Are you surprised? A lot of people think that when they become Christians everything will be good all the time, and bad things won't happen to them. But that's not true. The Bible never says that. Instead, the Bible tells us we will be persecuted.

Look back at 2 Timothy 3:13 WHAT do you learn about evil men and imposters? **They go from bad to worse, deceiving and being deceived.**

Way to go! Today you have seen how Timothy followed Paul's example, and you got a close-up look at some of Paul's persecutions, how he endured, and how God rescued him! You also saw that everyone who wants to live a godly life will be persecuted.

Continue in the Things You Have Learned   119

And you saw that evil men not only are deceived themselves but also deceive other people. Remember to follow Paul's example and avoid these people! All right! Hop on those bikes and get ready to race. Don't forget to practice your memory verse!

(page 119)

DAY FIVE
BREAKAWAY

91 What a bike race! You have pulled out of the pack and are now in the breakaway group. Keep on pedaling. You are doing great. One more turn and you should be headed downhill. Don't give up!

Look at Sam. He's cheering you on as he rides on Coach Neighbors's motorcycle behind the racers. You did it! You continued your pace and crossed the finish line for a bronze medal. Way to hang in there and win another medal!

Now let's find out how we can continue in the things we have learned to earn a medal as God's champion. Ask God for His help.

Then turn to page 164 and read 2 Timothy 3:14-17. Ask the 5 W's and an H.

(page 164)

deceiving and being deceived.

92 14 You, however, continue in the things you have learned and become convinced of, knowing from whom you have learned them,

15 and that from childhood you have known the sacred writings which are able to give you the wisdom that leads to salvation through faith which is in Christ Jesus.

16 All Scripture is inspired by God and profitable for teaching, for reproof, for correction, for training in righteousness;

17 so that the man of God may be adequate, equipped for every good work.

Guided Instruction

Ask God to help you become one of His champions.

91 Turn to page 119 and read "Breakaway."

92 Turn to page 164 and reread 2 Timothy 3:14-17 to answer the questions.

Guided Instruction

2 Timothy 3:14 WHAT was Timothy to do? Continue in things he learned

2 Timothy 1:5 WHO in Timothy's family had a sincere faith? WHO taught Timothy? His grandmother Lois and his mother Eunice

2 Timothy 3:15 WHAT did Timothy learn? The sacred writings

2 Timothy 3:15 WHEN did he learn the sacred writings? As a child

2 Timothy 3:15 WHAT are the sacred writings able to give you? Wisdom

2 Timothy 3:15 WHAT does wisdom lead to? Salvation

2 Timothy 3:15 HOW do you receive salvation? Through faith in Christ Jesus

---

120   WEEK FIVE

2 Timothy 3:14 WHAT was Timothy to do?
Continue in things he learned

Did you remember to put a green box around this instruction?

Look back at 2 Timothy 1:5 WHO in Timothy's family had a sincere faith? WHO taught Timothy?
His grandmother Lois and his mother Eunice

2 Timothy 3:15 WHAT did Timothy learn?
The sacred writings

2 Timothy 3:15 WHEN did he learn the sacred writings?
As a child

Did you put a pink cloud around this encouragement from Paul?

2 Timothy 3:15 WHAT are the sacred writings able to give you?
Wisdom

2 Timothy 3:15 WHAT does wisdom lead to?
Salvation

2 Timothy 3:15 HOW do you receive salvation?
Through faith in Christ Jesus

Isn't that awesome! Timothy was taught God's Word as a child. Paul is telling Timothy to continue in what he knows, the sacred writings, God's Word.

God's Word will help you recognize false teaching, it will get you through suffering and persecution, and it will show you how you are to live so you can please God! Remember, you have to know God's Word before you can pass it on to others. And just think—you are becoming a "Timothy" or a "Timeothea" (if you are a girl). You are learning God's Word right now while you are young!

WHAT else can we learn about the Word?

2 Timothy 3:16 WHAT do we see about all Scipture?

It is _____**inspired**_____ by God.

The Greek word for *inspired* is *theopneustos*. It is pronounced like this: *theh-op-nyoó-stos*. *Theos* means God, and *pneo* means to breathe. So the word *inspired* (*theopneustos*) means the Scripture is "God-breathed." This is the only place in the whole New Testament that this word is used. Look up and read 2 Peter 1:20-21.

HOW did we get the Scripture? HOW did men know

what to write? Men ___**moved**___ by the ___**Holy**___

___**Spirit**___ spoke from ___**God**___.

Isn't that awesome? We know we can trust what the Bible tells us because it comes directly from God.

2 Timothy 3:16 WHAT are the four things that the Scripture is profitable for?

1. **Teaching** _____

2. **Reproof** _____

3. **Correction** _____

4. **Training in righteousness** _____

The Bible doesn't contain God's words; it *is* the Word of God. It is "God-breathed" and is good for teaching (so we can know the truth), for reproof (so we can know when we are doing something wrong), for correction (so we can correct what we have

Guided Instruction

2 Timothy 3:16 WHAT do we see about all Scripture? It is <u>inspired</u> by God.

Discuss the Greek word for *inspired*.

Look up and read 2 Peter 1:20-21.

HOW did we get the Scripture? HOW did men know what to write? Men <u>moved</u> by the <u>Holy</u> <u>Spirit</u> spoke from <u>God</u>.

2 Timothy 3:16 WHAT are the four things that the Scripture is profitable for?

1. <u>Teaching</u>

2. <u>Reproof</u>

3. <u>Correction</u>

4. <u>Training in righteousness</u>

Guided Instruction

2 Timothy 3:17 WHY? So that the man of <u>God</u> may be <u>adequate</u>, <u>equipped</u> for every <u>good</u> <u>work</u>

93 Lead students through the application questions on page 122.

Say the memory verse out loud to a friend (Teacher Guide page 114).

Thank God for the privilege to learn more about Him and His awesome gift.

If you are a classroom teacher you may want to give your students a quiz on their memory verse. There is also a quiz on Week Five on page 159 to check memory and understanding.

This is a great time to review the whole week by playing a game.

Memory Verse

"You, however, continue in the things you have learned and become convinced of, knowing from whom you have learned them."

2 Timothy 3:14

---

122   WEEK FIVE

done wrong and know how to get it right), and for training in righteousness (so we can live right and have a right relationship with God).

2 Timothy 3:17 WHY? So that the man of ____God____ may be ____adequate____, ____equipped____ for every ____good____ ____work____.

That means we will be completely qualified so that we can do the work God has for us. We can live the way God wants us to live! Nothing is more important than knowing God's Word! Now ask yourself:

93
- Do you believe WHAT the Bible says? ____ Yes ____ No
- Will you choose to believe what the Bible says over what man says? ____ Yes ____ No
- Will you allow God's Word to show you where you are wrong? ____ Yes ____ No
- Are you willing to be corrected? Will you change what's wrong to what's right even if means changing what you believe? ____ Yes ____ No
- Are you willing to be trained in righteousness so God can use you for every good work? ____ Yes ____ No

What an awesome week! Are you willing to continue in the things that you know? WHO did you learn the sacred writings from?

_____

Why don't you tell that person thank you for teaching you God's Word. Now say your verse out loud to a grown-up so you can continue in the things you have learned and become God's champion!

6

PREACH THE GOSPEL

2 TIMOTHY 4

Wow! Can you believe that this is our last week at our summer sports camp? We have learned so much! Last week as we hit our target and raced on our bikes, we saw that we are living in the last days. And we saw how to spot some ungodly men and silly women who oppose the truth and deceive others.

We also saw how Paul was persecuted, how he endured, and how God rescued him. And we saw the importance of Scripture. The Bible doesn't contain God's words; it is the Word of God. It will teach us what is right and what is wrong, and show us how to do what God says is right! It will equip us to do God's work! *Awesome!* What will we discover as we read the final pages of Paul's letter? Let's find out.

94
DAY ONE
PRACTICE DRILLS

"All right!" Coach Neighbors gathered Team USA together. "Let's get to work on our Bible training. Then we need to head to

123

the soccer field and practice for tomorrow's game. Is everybody ready to find out how Paul ends his letter?"

"We sure are!" shouted Team USA.

"Great! Max, why don't you ask God to help us in our training so we can serve Him!"

Great! Now that we've asked for God's help, let's turn to page 164. Read 2 Timothy 4 and mark the key words listed below and any synonyms.

DAY ONE

What a study! Thank God for the privilege to delve into His Holy Word.

94 Turn to page 123 and read "2 Timothy 4" and "Practice Drills."

Guided Instruction

95 Add any new key words to your whiteboard and key word bookmark. Turn to page 164 and read 2 Timothy 4 aloud using your Observation Worksheet visual aid as students follow along and call out each key word. Then mark them together as we noted on p. 13.

God (draw a purple triangle and color it yellow)

Christ Jesus (Lord, Judge) (draw a purple cross and color it yellow)

Gospel (the word, sound doctrine, the truth, proclamation) (draw a red megaphone and color it green)

Turn away (turn aside) (draw a brown arch over the words)

Draw a green box around each instruction.

WHERE (double underline in green words that denote place)

WHEN (draw a green clock over words that denote time)

(page 124)

y synonyms.

God (draw a purple triangle and color it yellow)

Christ Jesus (Lord, Judge) (draw a purple cross and color it yellow)

gospel (and synonyms for the gospel: *the word* [verse 2], *sound doctrine* [verse 3], *the truth* [verse 4], *proclamation* [verse 17]) (draw a red megaphone like this: and color it green)

turn away (turn aside) (draw a brown arch over it like this: ⌒)

Look for any instructions to Timothy and draw a green box around each instruction.

Don't forget to mark your pronouns! And don't forget to double underline the WHERE in green and anything that tells you WHEN with a green clock 🕐 or green circle ○ .

Fantastic! Now, grab your soccer ball and work on your skills as you find the correct path on the soccer field maze. Figure out how to score a goal and solve this week's memory verse. Then fill in the blanks with the correct words on the lines underneath the soccer field.

(page 164)

Chapter 4

95 1 I solemnly charge you in the presence of God and of Christ Jesus, who is to judge the living and the dead, and by His appearing and His kingdom:

Observation Worksheets—2 Timothy 165

2 preach the word; be ready in season and out of season; reprove, rebuke, exhort, with great patience and instruction.

3 For the time will come when they will not endure sound doctrine; but wanting to have their ears tickled, they will accumulate for themselves teachers in accordance to their own desires,

4 and will turn away their ears from the truth and will turn aside to myths.

5 But you, be sober in all things, endure hardship, do the work of an evangelist, fulfill your ministry.

6 For I am already being poured out as a drink offering, and the time of my departure has come.

7 I have fought the good fight, I have finished the course, I have kept the faith;

(page 165)

Guided Instruction

8 in the future there is laid up for me the crown of righteousness, which the Lord, the righteous Judge, will award to me on that day; and not only to me, but also to all who have loved His appearing.

9 Make every effort to come to me soon;

10 for Demas, having loved this present world, has deserted me and gone to Thessalonica; Crescens has gone to Galatia, Titus to Dalmatia.

11 Only Luke is with me. Pick up Mark and bring him with you, for he is useful to me for service.

12 But Tychicus I have sent to Ephesus.

13 When you come bring the cloak which I left at Troas with Carpus, and the books, especially the parchments.

14 Alexander the coppersmith did me much harm; the Lord will repay him according to his deeds.

15 Be on guard against him yourself, for he vigorously opposed our teaching.

16 At my first defense no one supported me, but all deserted me; may it not be counted against them.

166　　　　*Observation Worksheets*

17 But the Lord stood with me and strengthened me, so that through me the proclamation might be fully accomplished, and that all the Gentiles might hear; and I was rescued out of the lion's mouth.

18 The Lord will rescue me from every evil deed, and will bring me safely to His heavenly kingdom; to Him be the glory forever and ever. Amen.

19 Greet Prisca and Aquila, and the household of Onesiphorus.

20 Erastus remained at Corinth, but Trophimus I left sick at Miletus.

21 Make every effort to come before winter. Eubulus greets you, also Pudens and Linus and Claudia and all the brethren.

22 The Lord be with your spirit. Grace be with you.

Guided Instruction

96 Find the correct path on the maze on page 125 to determine the memory verse.

<u>But</u> <u>you</u>, <u>be sober</u> <u>in</u> <u>all</u> <u>things</u>, <u>endure</u> <u>hardship</u>, <u>do the work</u> <u>of an evangelist</u>, <u>fulfill</u> <u>your</u> <u>ministry</u>.

2 Timothy 4:<u>5</u>

Copy the memory verse to an index card and practice saying it three times, three times a day.

Preach the Gospel　　　　125

But you, be sober in
all things, endure hardship,
do the work of an
evangelist, fulfill your
ministry.

2 Timothy 4: 5

Way to score! Don't forget to practice saying your verse out loud three times today!

126   WEEK SIX

DAY TWO

97

SHOOT!

"Molly, Max is wide open…pass it to Max," Coach Neighbors shouted across the soccer field. "Go, Max…way to take it down field. You've got it! Great pass. Morgan, take the shot! All right! Way to go, Team USA! Great shot, Morgan. Great assist, Max."

There goes the whistle, and it's another win for Team USA. Coach Neighbors hugged the kids as they ran off the field. "Way to play as a team instead of putting yourself first. Great pass, Molly. Max, I am so proud of the way you passed to Morgan instead of taking the shot. Way to go, Team! Let's hit the showers and get back to 2 Timothy."

What a great game! Ask God to help you be a good team player as a member of His team. Then turn to page 164 and read 2 Timothy 4:1-5.

Guided Instruction

DAY TWO

Ask God to keep you focused on His Word today.

97 Turn to page 126 and read "Shoot!"

Guided Instruction

98 Turn to page 164 and reread 2 Timothy 4:1-5 to answer the questions.

(page 164)

98

Chapter 4

1 I solemnly charge you in the presence of God and of Christ Jesus, who is to judge the living and the dead, and by His appearing and His kingdom:

Observation Worksheets—2 Timothy   165

2 preach the word; be ready in season and out of season; reprove, rebuke, exhort, with great patience and instruction.

3 For the time will come when they will not endure sound doctrine; but wanting to have their ears tickled, they will accumulate for themselves teachers in accordance to their own desires,

4 and will turn away their ears from the truth and will turn aside to myths.

5 But you, be sober in all things, endure hardship, do the work of an evangelist, fulfill your ministry.

6 For I am already being poured out as a drink offering, and the

Preach the Gospel   127

Let's ask the 5 W's and an H to find out what Paul's final words are to Timothy as he wraps up his letter.

(page 127)

2 Timothy 4:1 WHAT is Paul doing? WHAT does he say to Timothy?

I ____solemnly____ ____charge____ you

2 Timothy 4:1 In WHOSE presence does Paul make this charge?

_____**God and Christ Jesus**_____

Do you see the seriousness of this charge? Paul wanted Timothy to know how important his final words are.

2 Timothy 4:1 WHAT do we learn about Jesus in this verse?

He is to ____**judge**____ the ____**living**____ and the

---

128   WEEK SIX
_____

____**dead**____ by His ____**appearing**____
and His ____**kingdom**____.

Wow! When Jesus comes back, He is going to judge the living and the dead! Did you know that Christians will be judged? Second Corinthians 5:10 tells us we will all appear before the judgment seat of Christ for the things we have done, whether good or bad. We are saved by God's grace and will live with Jesus forever, but we are rewarded for our deeds.

Charging Timothy in God's presence is like standing before God and Jesus face-to-face. Every person will one day stand before God and Jesus either at the judgment seat of Christ, where Christians are judged (2 Corinthians 5:10); (Revelation 20:4-6), or at the Great White Throne judgment, where unbelievers (the dead) are judged (Revelation 20:11-12).

2 Timothy 4:2 WHAT is the charge? WHAT is Timothy to do?

Preach the Word
_____

Did you put a green box around this instruction?

WHAT does it mean to preach the word? The Greek word for *preach* is *kêrussô*. It is pronounced like this: *kay-roos-so*. It means to herald or proclaim the divine truth, the gospel.

In Paul's day, the rulers had heralds that made special announcements to the people in loud, clear voices so everyone could hear and heed the message. Timothy is to herald the gospel so the people can hear and heed it.

2 Timothy 4:2 WHEN is Timothy to be ready?

In season and out of season
_____

Guided Instruction

2 Timothy 4:1 WHAT is Paul doing? WHAT does he say to Timothy? I solemnly charge you.

2 Timothy 4:1 In WHOSE presence does Paul make this charge? God and Christ Jesus

2 Timothy 4:1 WHAT do we learn about Jesus in this verse? He is to judge the living and the dead by His appearing and His kingdom.

Read and discuss the text below this verse.

2 Timothy 4:2 WHAT is the charge? WHAT is Timothy to do? Preach the Word

2 Timothy 4:2 WHEN is Timothy to be ready? In season and out of season

Guided Instruction

2 Timothy 4:2 HOW is he to preach the word? He is to <u>reprove</u>, <u>rebuke</u>, <u>exhort</u>, with great <u>patience</u> and <u>instruction</u>.

2 Timothy 4:3 WHY is it so important to know the truth? WHAT will happen in time? A time will come when they <u>will not endure sound doctrine</u>.

2 Timothy 4:3 WHAT will they want instead of sound doctrine? <u>To have their ears tickled</u>

2 Timothy 4:3 WHAT will they accumulate for themselves? <u>Teachers in accordance with their own desires</u>

(page 128)

That means Timothy is to preach the gospel when it is convenient and when it isn't. Paul always found an opportunity to share the Word whether he was in the temple, in the courts, or on the stormy sea. Paul was telling Timothy to use every opportunity to preach the Word and not to make excuses about it not being a good time or a good place.

Preach the Gospel   129

Remember, Timothy is living in a time when Christians are being persecuted. It is not an easy time to share the gospel, but Paul charges him in God and Jesus' presence that Timothy is to preach the gospel at all times!

2 Timothy 4:2 HOW is he to preach the word?

He is to ____**reprove**____, ____**rebuke**____, ____**exhort**____, with great ____**patience**____ and ____**instruction**____.

To reprove means to tell someone he is doing something wrong. To rebuke is to admonish and warn someone. And you already know that to exhort is to encourage.

Timothy is preach the Word at all times, telling others what they are doing wrong, warning them, and encouraging them. He is to be patient and give them the right teaching. Timothy is to guard the treasure. He needs to make sure others know the truth of the gospel.

2 Timothy 4:3 WHY is it so important to know the truth? WHAT will happen in time?

For a time will come when they ____**will**____ ____**not**____ ____**endure**____ ____**sound**____ ____**doctrine**____.

2 Timothy 4:3 WHAT will they want instead of sound (healthy) doctrine (teaching)?
____**To have their ears tickled**____

2 Timothy 4:3 WHAT will they accumulate for themselves?
<u>**Teachers in accordance with their own desires**</u>

130   WEEK SIX

2 Timothy 4:4 WHAT will they turn their ears away from?

Truth

2 Timothy 4:4 WHAT will they turn to?

Myths

Whoa, do you see how bad these last days are? A time will come when people will no longer want the truth but will want to have their ears tickled. Tickling your ear feels good. Here, it means telling people things that make them feel good but that aren't good for them. That means people will want teachers and preachers who tell them what they want to hear instead of the truth. That way, they can do what they want to do and not have someone correct and admonish them.

HOW does this compare to our world today? Do we have false teachers? _____ Do you know people who don't want to know the truth so they can live any way they want to? _____

> WHY is it so important for Timothy to preach the Word in these last days? WHY is it so important for us to know and teach the truth?
>
> _____
>
> _____

2 Timothy 4:5 WHAT does Paul tell Timothy to do?

Be sober in all things, endure hardship, do the work of an evangelist, and fulfill your ministry.

Did you put a green box around the instructions?

Paul tells Timothy to be watchful, to be serious about his work, to endure hardships, to do the work of an evangelist. An evangelist is someone who shares the gospel. You can be an evangelist by telling kids at school or in your neighborhood about Jesus.

Guided Instruction

2 Timothy 4:4 WHAT will they turn their ears away from? <u>Truth</u>

2 Timothy 4:4 WHAT will they turn to? <u>Myths</u>

Discuss the personal application questions. Have students respond.

2 Timothy 4:5 WHAT does Paul tell Timothy to do? <u>Be sober in all things, endure hardship, do the work of an evangelist, and fulfill your ministry.</u>

Read and discuss the rest of the text on pages 130-131.

Guided Instruction

Practice saying the memory verse (Teacher Guide page 134).

You could take a mission trip to another city in the U.S. or in another country. On your mission trip, you could share the gospel with others as you help build a school or a church. You could teach kids to study the Bible the same way you do. You could tell them how you came to know Jesus, feed the poor, and help those who are sick.

You can share the gospel in lots of ways. Timothy is to fulfill his ministry, to do the work God has for him to do. God has a ministry for each one of us to fulfill. We all have different gifts, and God will use us in many different ways.

WHAT are your gifts? Do you like to teach, sing, draw, play sports, work with your hands, cook, create, write, learn, or help others?

Write out what your gifts are.

_____

God will use some of us to teach and some of us to take care of our homes and raise godly families. Some of us will care for the sick, some will work in a business, some will serve others, some will go on the mission field; and some will know that their mission field is in their own neighborhood or school. What we do doesn't matter as long as we follow God and use our gifts to serve Him. And regardless of what our gifts are, we all have one thing that we are to do, and that's to share the good news about Jesus with others.

How can God use you? _____

_____

Awesome! Now, don't forget to practice your memory verse!

DAY THREE
SLIDE TACKLE

"All right, Wes!" Coach Neighbors patted Wes's back as he came out for a break. "That was a great slide tackle. Way to get the ball back. Come on, Josh, get it to Max. Shoot, Max, shoot!"

Did you see that? Max shot the winning goal for Team USA! We have two more games to play to find out who wins the gold medal. Aren't you excited? Let's head to our team meeting and find out what Paul has to say to Timothy.

Talk to God. Then turn to page 165. Read 2 Timothy 4:6-8 and ask the 5 W's and an H.

(page 165)

99 6 For I am already being poured out as a drink offering, and the time of my departure has come.

7 I have fought the good fight, I have finished the course, I have kept the faith;

8 in the future there is laid up for me the crown of righteousness, which the Lord, the righteous Judge, will award to me on that day; and not only to me, but also to all who have loved His appearing.

9 Make every effort to come to me soon;

Guided Instruction

DAY THREE

Ask God to fill you with clear understanding of His Word.

99 Turn to page 165 and read 2 Timothy 4:6-8 to answer the questions.

Guided Instruction

2 Timothy 4:6 WHAT do we see about Paul? He is being poured out as a drink offering.

2 Timothy 4:6 WHAT is it time for? Paul's departure

2 Timothy 4:7 WHAT does Paul say about himself? He fought the good fight, finished the course. He kept the faith.

2 Timothy 4:8 WHAT will Paul receive in the future? A crown of righteousness

2 Timothy 4:8 WHO will award this crown to Paul? The Lord

2 Timothy 4:8 WHEN will he receive this crown? On that day

2 Timothy 4:8 Is Paul the only one to receive this crown? No

WHO else receives this crown? All who love His appearing

(page 132)

2 Timothy 4:6 WHAT do we see about Paul?

He is being poured out as a drink offering.

Paul uses this description of the Old Testament drink offering being poured out as a sacrifice to show that his life is being poured out. He is giving his life as a sacrifice for Jesus.

2 Timothy 4:6 WHAT is it time for?

Paul's departure

Paul knows he is going to die. He is going home to heaven to be with God and Jesus.

2 Timothy 4:7 WHAT does Paul say about himself?
He fought the good fight, finished the course.
He kept the faith.

2 Timothy 4:8 WHAT will Paul receive in the future?
A crown of righteousness

Preach the Gospel   133

2 Timothy 4:8 WHO will award this crown to Paul?
The Lord

2 Timothy 4:8 WHEN will he receive this crown?
On that day

2 Timothy 4:8 Is Paul the only one to receive this crown?
No

WHO else receives this crown?
All who love His appearing

Wow! We have seen in Revelation 22:12 that when Jesus comes back, His reward will be with Him. Now we see what one of those rewards is—the crown of righteousness that is given to those who have loved Jesus' appearing.

Last week we drew a picture of Paul's persecutions. Today let's draw a picture in the box below to show Paul's reward for fighting the good fight and finishing the course. Draw a picture of Paul receiving the crown of righteousness from Jesus.

(page 133)

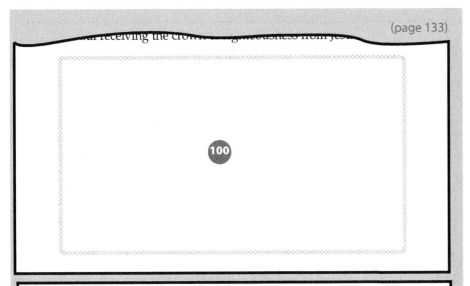

134   WEEK SIX

Does the Bible talk about crowns in any other places? WHAT other crowns are there?

Look up and read James 1:12. WHAT is this crown?

<u>**The crown of life**</u>

HOW do you get it? **Persevere under trials and love the Lord**

Look up and read Revelation 2:10. WHAT crown is given?   **The crown of life**

Look up and read 1 Peter 5:4. WHAT crown will be given when the Chief Shepherd (Jesus) appears?

The unfading crown of glory

This crown is for the shepherd of the flock. It is a crown that will be given to pastors.

Look up and read 1 Thessalonians 2:19. WHAT is the crown in this verse? The crown of <u>**exultation**</u>.

Guided Instruction

100 Draw a picture of Paul receiving the crown of righteousness in the box on page 133.

What other crowns are there? Look up and read the selected verses to answer the questions.

James 1:12 WHAT is this crown? <u>The crown of life</u>

HOW do you get it? <u>Persevere under trials and love the Lord</u>

Revelation 2:10 WHAT crown is given? <u>The crown of life</u>

1 Peter 5:4 WHAT crown will be given when the Chief Shepherd (Jesus) appears? <u>The unfading crown of glory</u>

1 Thessalonians 2:19 WHAT is the crown in this verse? The crown of <u>exultation</u>

Read and discuss the rest of the text for this lesson.

Practice saying the memory verse with a friend (Teacher Guide page 134).

Guided Instruction

Wow! Just look at all you have seen today. You have seen that Paul is being poured out as a drink offering. He is giving his life as a sacrifice for Jesus.

Paul is about to die. He will depart from this world to spend eternity with Jesus. As Paul prepares to die, he looks back at his life. Look at what he says about himself: "I have fought the good fight." Like a boxer, he has given his best in the contest. " I have finished the course." Like a runner in a race, he has obeyed the rules, he finished the race, and now will receive a prize. "I have kept the faith." Paul has guarded the treasure that God gave him.

After Paul looks back, he looks ahead to the future at the crown he will receive because he has been faithful. Paul has lived his life for Jesus! He will receive the prize of an imperishable crown (1 Corinthians 9:25).

Amazing! Are you going to live your life so you can receive the prize? Will Jesus reward you with one of these awesome crowns so you can lay it at His feet to thank Him for all He's done for you?

Don't forget to practice your memory verse.

(page 135)

DAY FOUR
DEFEND THE GOAL

(101) "Way to defend the goal, Matthew!" Coach Neighbors called out from the sidelines. "Okay, let's have a good throw-in. Good, good. Dribble that ball. Bethany, take it. Okay, Max, shoot! All right! One more goal for Team USA. You can do it!

"Here it comes. Matthew, be ready; defend the goal. All right! Way to kick it out of there. Take it Molly. Run, Molly, run—take it all the way. Pass—Josh is open. Shoot, Josh! You did it! Three to two! You just defeated Team Greece. Only one more game to a gold medal."

136   WEEK SIX

What an incredible day for Team USA. Let's get our minds focused to prepare for tomorrow's deciding game by doing our training in 2 Timothy. Don't forget to pray. Turn to page 165 and read 2 Timothy 4:9-22.

Let's take a look at Paul's last words. Ask the 5 W's and an H

(page 165)

and not only to me, but also to all who have loved His appearing.

(102) 9 | Make every effort to come to me soon; |

10 for Demas, having loved this present world, has deserted me and gone to Thessalonica; Crescens has gone to Galatia, Titus to Dalmatia.

11 Only Luke is with me. Pick up Mark and bring him with you, for he is useful to me for service.

12 But Tychicus I have sent to Ephesus.

13 When you come bring the cloak which I left at Troas with Carpus, and the books, especially the parchments.

14 Alexander the coppersmith did me much harm; the Lord will repay him according to his deeds.

15 | Be on guard against him yourself, | for he vigorously opposed our teaching.

16 At my first defense no one supported me, but all deserted me; may it not be counted against them.

Guided Instruction

DAY FOUR

Ask God to give you clarity to understand this lesson.

(101) Turn to page 135 and read "Defend the Goal."

(102) Turn to page 165 and read 2 Timothy 4:9-22 to answer the questions.

Guided Instruction

2 Timothy 4:9 WHAT is Paul's instruction? "Make every <u>effort</u> to <u>come</u> to me <u>soon</u>."

2 Timothy 4:10 WHAT did we learn about Demas? Demas <u>loved</u> this present <u>world</u>. He <u>deserted</u> Paul and went to Thessalonica.

2 Timothy 4:11 WHAT do we see about Luke? Luke is <u>with</u> <u>me</u>.

2 Timothy 4:11 WHY does Paul want Timothy to pick up Mark? "For he is <u>useful</u> to me for <u>service</u>."

2 Timothy 4:13 WHAT does Paul want Timothy to bring? The <u>cloak</u> and the <u>books</u>, especially the <u>parchment</u>

---

166   *Observation Worksheets*

17 But the Lord stood with me and strengthened me, so that through me the proclamation might be fully accomplished, and that all the Gentiles might hear; and I was rescued out of the lion's mouth.

18 The Lord will rescue me from every evil deed, and will bring me safely to His heavenly kingdom; to Him be the glory forever and ever. Amen.

19 Greet Prisca and Aquila, and the household of Onesiphorus.

20 Erastus remained at Corinth, but Trophimus I left sick at Miletus.

21 Make every effort to come before winter. Eubulus greets you, also Pudens and Linus and Claudia and all the brethren.

22 The Lord be with your spirit. Grace be with you.

---

2 Timothy 4:9-22.   (page 136)

Let's take a look at Paul's last words. Ask the 5 W's and an H to find out what Paul says next.

2 Timothy 4:9 WHAT is Paul's instruction?

"Make every ____**effort**____ to ____**come**____ to me ____**soon**____."

Did you put a green box around this instruction?

2 Timothy 4:10 WHAT did we learn about Demas?

Demas ____**loved**____ this present ____**world**____. He ____**deserted**____ Paul and went to Thessalonica.

2 Timothy 4:11 WHAT do we see about Luke?

Luke is ____**with**____ ____**me**____.

2 Timothy 4:11 WHY does Paul want Timothy to pick up Mark?

"For he is ____**useful**____ to me for ____**service**____."

2 Timothy 4:13 WHAT does Paul want Timothy to bring?

The ____**cloak**____ and the ____**books**____, especially the ____**parchment**____.

2 Timothy 4:14 WHAT do we see about Alexander the coppersmith?

He did Paul much _____harm_____.

WHAT will the Lord do?

The Lord will _____repay_____ him according to his _____deeds_____.

2 Timothy 4:15 WHAT did Paul tell Timothy to do?

_____Be_____ on _____guard_____ against him.

WHY? Because he vigorously _____opposed_____ Paul's _____teaching_____.

2 Timothy 4:16 WHAT happened at Paul's first defense?

No one _____supported_____ Paul but _____all_____ _____deserted_____ him.

2 Timothy 4:17 WHO stood with Paul?

The _____Lord_____

2 Timothy 4:17 WHAT did the Lord do?

He _____strengthened_____ Paul.

WHY? So that the _____proclamation_____ might be fully _____accomplished_____ and that all the Gentiles might _____hear_____.

Wow! God gave Paul strength so that all the Gentiles could hear the gospel!

2 Timothy 4:17 WHAT do we see about Paul?

Guided Instruction

2 Timothy 4:14 WHAT do we see about Alexander of the coppersmith? He did Paul much <u>harm</u>.

WHAT will the Lord do? The Lord will <u>repay</u> him according to his <u>deeds</u>.

2 Timothy 4:15 WHAT did Paul tell Timothy to do? <u>Be</u> on <u>guard</u> against him.

WHY? Because he vigorously <u>opposed</u> Paul's <u>teaching</u>.

2 Timothy 4:16 WHAT happened at Paul's first defense? No one <u>supported</u> Paul but <u>all</u> <u>deserted</u> him.

2 Timothy 4:17 WHO stood with Paul? The <u>Lord</u>

2 Timothy 4:17 WHAT did the Lord do? He <u>strengthened</u> Paul.

WHY? So that the <u>proclamation</u> might be fully <u>accomplished</u> and that all the Gentiles might <u>hear</u>

Guided Instruction

2 Timothy 4:17 WHAT do we see about Paul? He was <u>rescued</u> out of the <u>lion's mouth</u>.

2 Timothy 4:18 WHAT will the Lord do? He will <u>rescue</u> Paul from every <u>evil deed</u> and will <u>bring</u> him <u>safely</u> to His <u>heavenly</u> <u>kingdom</u>.

2 Timothy 4:21 WHAT is Paul's instruction? Make every <u>effort</u> to <u>come</u> before <u>winter</u>.

Is this the same instruction in 4:9? <u>Yes</u>

Turn to page 160 and read 2 Timothy 1:4 to answer the next questions.

2 Timothy 1:4 WHAT is Paul longing for? To <u>see</u> Timothy

Return to 2 Timothy 4:22 to answer the next question.

2 Timothy 4:22 WHAT does Paul ask for? HOW does he close his letter? The Lord be with your <u>spirit</u>. <u>Grace</u> be with you.

WHO stood up with Paul? <u>The Lord</u>

138   WEEK SIX

He was <u>rescued</u> out of the <u>lion's</u> <u>mouth</u>.

2 Timothy 4:18 WHAT will the Lord do?

He will <u>rescue</u> Paul from every <u>evil</u> <u>deed</u> and will <u>bring</u> him <u>safely</u> to His <u>heavenly</u> <u>kingdom</u>.

2 Timothy 4:21 WHAT is Paul's instruction?

Make every <u>effort</u> to <u>come</u> before <u>winter</u>.

Does this sound like the same instruction in 4:9? <u>Yes</u>

Did you put a green box around it?

Turn to page 160 and look at 2 Timothy 1:4. WHAT is Paul longing for? To <u>see</u> Timothy.

Paul says this three times. He really wants to see his beloved son in the faith before he dies.

2 Timothy 4:22 WHAT does Paul ask for? HOW does he close his letter?

The Lord be with your <u>spirit</u>. <u>Grace</u> be with you.

Wow! What an awesome letter! Paul is suffering in prison for the gospel. He knows his time is short. He knows he is going to die soon. Paul wants Timothy to pick up Mark and come see him before the winter. He is alone; only Luke is with him. All of the others have deserted him. And Alexander did him harm!

But look at WHO stood with Paul, who rescued him and strengthened him? WHO was it? <u>The Lord</u>

Content

God never left Paul. Do you know that Hebrews 13:5 tells us that God will never leave or forsake us? He keeps His Word! God was with Paul, rescuing him from every evil deed. And Paul knows that God will bring him safely home. Heaven is our real home, our forever home. How amazing is that? Look at how much God loves you! We may go through trials and suffering, but we are never alone. God is with us. Our divine Coach will always be with us. He will strengthen us and bring us safely to His kingdom!

Now, go back and find all the words in each blank and circle each one of these words in the word search below. And if a word is used more than once, circle it just one time.

Great work! Don't forget to practice your memory verse.

Guided Instruction

Find all of the underlined words and circle them in the word search on page 139.

Practice saying the memory verse with a friend (Teacher Guide page 134).

Guided Instruction

DAY FIVE

Ask God to lead you as you study this last lesson on Timothy.

104 Turn to page 140 and read "Going for Gold!"

105 Turn to page 164 and read 2 Timothy 4 to complete the chart below.

Characteristics of a Believer

2 Timothy 4:2 Preach the word; be ready in season and out of season. Reprove, rebuke, exhort, with great patience and instruction.

2 Timothy 4:5 Be sober in all things, endure hardship, do the work of an evangelist, fulfill your ministry.

---

140   WEEK SIX

DAY FIVE

104

GOING FOR GOLD!

"Good kick, Matthew," Coach Neighbors called out. "Be ready, team. Here they come. Go for the ball, Wes. Pass it to Morgan. Turn, Morgan, turn! There goes the two-minute warning. Come on, Team USA, you can do it! Don't give up—hang in there!"

Coach Neighbors held his breath as Team Brazil headed toward the goal. Josh ran in and intercepted the ball. "All right! All right! Go, Molly! Pass it to Max. Take it, Max. Way to change direction. Great pass. Shoot, Morgan, shoot. You did it! Oh, man—you did it! You won the gold!"

Incredible! Why don't we shoot for gold as we finish up our training in 2 Timothy. Ask God to help you live out your life so that others see Jesus in you!

We're ready to finish our last day. Let's read 2 Timothy 4 and look for the characteristics of a believer—a faithful follower of Christ—and the characteristics of an unbeliever.

Turn to page 164 and read 2 Timothy 4. Look at each verse and fill in the characteristics of a believer in the chart below.

105

Characteristics of a Believer

2 Timothy 4:2 __Preach__ the __word__; be __ready__ __in__ season and __out__ of season. __Reprove__, __rebuke__, __exhort__, with great __patience__ and __instruction__.

2 Timothy 4:5 Be __sober__ in all __things__, __endure__ __hardship__, do the __work__

of an _____evangelist_____, _____fulfill_____ your _____ministry_____.

2 Timothy 4:7 Fight the _____good_____ _____fight_____, _____finish_____ the _____course_____, keep the _____faith_____.

2 Timothy 4:8 Will receive the _____crown_____ of _____righteousness_____, loves Jesus' _____appearing_____.

Now, read through the verses again. Look for the characteristics of an unbeliever and fill in the chart below.

Characteristics of an Unbeliever

106

2 Timothy 4:3 They will not _____endure_____ _____sound_____ _____doctrine_____. They will want to have their _____ears_____ tickled. They will accumulate _____teachers_____ in accordance to their own _____desires_____.

Guided Instruction

2 Timothy 4:7 Fight the <u>good</u> <u>fight</u>, <u>finish</u> the <u>course</u>, keep the <u>faith</u>.

2 Timothy 4:8 Will receive the <u>crown</u> of <u>righteousness</u>, loves Jesus' appearing.

106 Complete the chart of the characteristics of the unbeliever.

Characteristics of an Unbeliever

2 Timothy 4:3 They will not <u>endure</u> <u>sound</u> <u>doctrine</u>. They will want to have their <u>ears</u> tickled. They will accumulate <u>teachers</u> in accordance to their own <u>desires</u>.

Guided Instruction

2 Timothy 4:4 They will <u>turn</u> <u>away</u> their <u>ears</u> from the <u>truth</u> and will <u>turn</u> <u>aside</u> to <u>myths</u>.

2 Timothy 4:10 They will <u>love</u> this present <u>world</u>.

2 Timothy 4:14 They will do <u>harm</u>.

Say the memory verse to a grown-up (Teacher Guide page 134).

Read and discuss the rest of the text for this lesson.

Do the *Just for Fun* game on page 144.

Thank God for the privilege of studying His Word. He sees your heart and is pleased.

Play a game to review all of 2 Timothy.

If you are a classroom teacher you may want to give your students a quiz on their memory verse. There is also a quiz on Week Six on page 160 to check memory and understanding and a Final Exam to review the entire book on page 161.

If you are a Sunday School teacher this is a great time to review the whole week by playing a game like *The Matching Game* on page 164 or the *M&M® Draw Game* on page 165. This is also a great way for classroom teachers and homeschool families to review with students what they learned this week.

Memory Verse

"But you, be sober in all things, endure hardship, do the work of an evangelist, fulfill your ministry."

2 Timothy 4:5

---

2 Timothy 4:4 They will __turn__ __away__ their __ears__ from the __truth__ and will __turn__ __aside__ to __myths__.

2 Timothy 4:10 They will __love__ this present __world__.

2 Timothy 4:14 They will do __harm__.

All right! You have completed your charts, studied the whole book of 2 Timothy, and seen the characteristics of a true believer (a vessel of honor) and the characteristics of an unbeliever (a vessel of dishonor). Now ask yourself, *WHERE do I fit? Do my actions show that I am a believer? Can others tell by looking at my life that I am different, that I love Jesus?*

Think about what your actions show others. If you need to work on something or change something, go to God and ask Him to help you! Incredible! Find a grown-up, say that last memory verse, and determine to live it out in your life!

Now walk up to the platform. Stand tall and get ready to receive your gold medal. What an amazing performance! You are a true champion for God!

The Closing Ceremony

All right! You did it! You have trained hard, you have finished the course, and you have kept the faith to become a true champion for God! As we participate in the closing ceremony of our summer games, think about all you have learned.

You know that Paul is about to die. He is in prison, suffering for the gospel. But instead of feeling sorry for himself or worrying about his circumstances, Paul writes a letter to Timothy to encourage, instruct, warn, and charge Timothy.

Paul reminds Timothy to stir up the gift that God has given him, to fulfill the call that God has on his life. How about you? Do you know that God has a call on your life too?

You saw Paul tell Timothy not to be ashamed of the gospel, to join him in suffering for the gospel, to retain the standard of sound words, to guard the treasure, and to entrust the gospel to faithful men. *Wow!*

And what did you discover the gospel is? You saw it is revealed through Jesus Christ, and believing the gospel is the only way you can have eternal life. Have you accepted Jesus' awesome gift? Are you ready to share it with others?

You also discovered that you are to be a vessel of honor, careful about whom you hang out with, separating yourself from vessels of dishonor. You are to flee wrong things and pursue righteousness, faith, love, and peace. You are to be careful how you handle God's Word, and you saw that God's Word will equip you to do His work! *Amazing!* We are so proud of you!

Remember, we are living in the last days. Avoid ungodly men, continue in the things you have learned, and be ready to preach the Word at all times!

Here come Max, Molly, and Sam. Max has the baton. Are you ready? Start running, put your hand back… here it comes. Whack! Right into the palm of your hand. Now, hold it tight. Retain it. Guard it. Keep your head down and *run!* You

Guided Instruction

Guided Instruction

can do it! Don't give up! Pass it on! You are a champion! You can win the gold for God!

Molly, Max, and

(Sam)

P.S. Don't forget to fill out the card in the back of this book. We have something special to send you for finishing the course and keeping the faith! We hope you'll join us for another adventure in God's Word real soon!

P.S.S. Max and Molly have a game you might want to play called Believers or Unbelievers.

Just for Fun

You can play Max and Molly's game, Believers or Unbelievers, by yourself or with a friend or family member.

You'll need the game board on page 145, Believers and Unbelievers cards on page 147 and 148 (you'll need to cut those out), a coin to flip, and a marker for each player.

How to play: Place the Believers and Unbelievers cards facedown in the square provided on the game board. Start with your marker on the Start circle. Flip a coin. Heads you move two spaces. Tails you move one space. If you land on a space marked BUB (Believers or Unbelievers), pick up the top card from the pile and follow the instructions. Then return the card to the bottom of the pile. Have fun!

D4Y "Becoming God's Champion" Quizzes

Week 1: Guard the Treasure

1. Who wrote the letters to Timothy?
   a. Peter
   b. Paul
   c. James
   d. Mark

2. Who was an apostle of Christ Jesus?
   a. Herod
   b. John the Baptist
   c. Paul
   d. Pilate

3. Paul is _____ for the gospel.
   a. suffering
   b. singing
   c. playing
   d. waiting

4. Who is the Lord's prisoner in this epistle?
   a. Paul
   b. Timothy
   c. James
   d. Mark

5. What has been entrusted to Timothy?
   a. The religion
   b. The treasure
   c. A promise
   d. The parchment

6. Who refreshed Paul?
   a. James
   b. Mark
   c. Onesiphorus
   d. Eunice

7. What crown will Paul receive in the future?
   a. righteousness
   b. happiness
   c. purity
   d. jewels

8. A time will come when some will not _____ sound doctrine.
   a. ignore
   b. endure
   c. disbelieve
   d. hate

9. What should we do with such men?
   a. Befriend them
   b. Love them
   c. Avoid them
   d. Doubt them

10. What should Timothy not be ashamed of?
    a. Paul's reputation
    b. The testimony of Jesus
    c. His old age
    d. His physical health

Memory Verse

2 Timothy 1:14

"Guard through the Holy Spirit who dwells in us the treasure which has been entrusted to you."

Week 2: Don't Be Ashamed

1. What does each believer receive?
   a. A special gift
   b. Money
   c. Clothes
   d. Friends

2. What spirit has God not given us?
   a. Joy
   b. Timidity
   c. Peace
   d. Love

3. Where do we get our power from?
   a. The sun
   b. The Holy Spirit
   c. Our friends
   d. Our education

4. Who did God send for the propitiation for our sins?
   a. Paul
   b. Timothy
   c. Jesus
   d. Mark

5. What will Jesus be to the person who is ashamed of the Gospel?
   a. Ashamed
   b. Proud
   c. Happy
   d. Joyful

6. What did Paul instruct Timothy to do with the standard of sound words?
   a. Forget them
   b. Ignore them
   c. Retain them
   d. Change them

7. Who enables us to guard the treasure?
   a. The Holy Spirit
   b. Paul
   c. Parents
   d. Friends

8. God saved us through _____ granted to us in Christ Jesus.
   a. time
   b. works
   c. grace
   d. the Law

9. What did our Savior Christ Jesus do to death?
   a. Abolished it
   b. Strengthened it
   c. Sold it
   d. Forgave it

10. What is the free gift of God?
    a. Freedom to do anything we want
    b. Money
    c. Eternal life
    d. Unbelieving friends

Memory Verse

2 Timothy 1:9

"Who has saved us and called us with a holy calling, not according to our works, but according to His own purpose and grace which was granted us in Christ Jesus from all eternity."

Week 3: Entrust to Faithful Men

1. What did Paul tell Timothy to do in the grace of Jesus?
   a. Be strong
   b. Be happy
   c. Be safe
   d. Be relieved

2. Faithful men will be able to _____ others.
   a. love
   b. help
   c. teach
   d. meet

3. What is Timothy to do with Paul?
   a. Teach
   b. Suffer hardship
   c. Eat
   d. Help

4. How is Timothy to suffer hardship with Paul?
   a. Like a friend
   b. Like a teacher
   c. Like a good soldier of Christ
   d. Like a parent

5. What does Jesus have when He comes?
   a. Rewards
   b. Money
   c. Frustration
   d. Toys

6. Each man will be given his reward according to what he has _____.
   a. thought
   b. wished
   c. done
   d. felt

7. Salvation is in WHOM?
   a. Christ Jesus
   b. Preachers
   c. Teachers
   d. Judges

8. If we die in Christ, we will _____with Him.
   a. talk
   b. live
   c. die
   d. teach

9. What will we do with Jesus for 1000 years?
   a. Hunt
   b. Eat
   c. Reign
   d. Fish

10. What will He do if we deny Him?
    a. Forget us
    b. Save us
    c. Deny us
    d. Ignore us

Memory Verse

2 Timothy 2:15

"Be diligent to present yourself approved to God as a workman who does not need to be ashamed, accurately handling the word of truth."

Week 4: Handle God's Word Accurately

1. What does an *unbeliever* do with Christ?
   a. Deny Him
   b. Love Him
   c. Praise Him
   d. Serve Him

2. Paul told Timothy that it is useless to _____ about words.
   a. tell
   b. wrangle
   c. test
   d. forget

3. How is Timothy to present himself to God?
   a. Dirty
   b. Lukewarm
   c. Approved
   d. Faithless

4. If a workman accurately handles the word of truth, he won't be _____.
   a. ashamed
   b. proud
   c. indifferent
   d. forgiven

5. Unbelievers' evil speech spreads like _____.
   a. water
   b. oil
   c. gangrene
   d. butter

6. We are to be vessels of _____.
   a. honor
   b. cleanness
   c. truth
   d. works

7. The Lord's bond-servant is not to be _____.
   a. faithless
   b. quarrelsome
   c. reckless
   d. loud

8. With gentleness we are to _____ those in opposition.
   a. get
   b. leave
   c. correct
   d. ignore

9. The believer is to abstain from _____.
   a. wickedness
   b. truth
   c. peace
   d. kindness

10. A vessel of honor _____ himself.
    a. likes
    b. dresses
    c. cleanses
    d. presents

Memory Verse

2 Timothy 2:22

"Now flee from youthful lusts and pursue righteousness, faith, love and peace, with those who call on the Lord with a pure heart."

Week 5: Continue in the Things You Have Learned

1. We need to realize that _____times will come.
   a. difficult
   b. fruitful
   c. happy
   d. sad

2. How should children be toward their parents?
   a. Rebellious
   b. Obedient
   c. Indifferent
   d. Angry

3. What will God do if we confess our sins?
   a. Be happy
   b. Forgive us
   c. Help us
   d. Bless us

4. What does Paul say that we should hold?
   a. Godlessness
   b. Possessions
   c. Godliness
   d. Lies

5. What do unfaithful men do with the truth?
   a. Oppose it
   b. Love it
   c. Accept it
   d. Nothing

6. What are we to do with such men?
   a. Befriend them
   b. Pray against them
   c. Avoid them
   d. Hang out with them

7. At Antioch, Paul was persecuted and _____.
   a. suffered
   b. promoted
   c. hired
   d. worshipped

8. What did God do for Paul?
   a. Forgot him
   b. Left him alone
   c. Rescued him
   d. Discouraged him

9. What kind of writings did Timothy learn from Lois and Eunice?
   a. Sacred
   b. Funny
   c. False
   d. Kind

10. Timothy learned these writings as a(n) _____.
    a. adult
    b. child
    c. teenage
    d. librarian

Memory Verse

2 Timothy 3:14

"You, however, continue in the things you have learned and become convinced of, knowing from whom you have learned them."

Week 6: Preach the Gospel

1. Who will judge the living and the dead?
   a. Jesus
   b. Moses
   c. Abraham
   d. Mark

2. What is Timothy charged to do with the Word?
   a. Rewrite it
   b. Preach it
   c. Hide it
   d. Ignore it

3. What is Timothy to do in season and out of season?
   a. Be happy
   b. Be ready to preach
   c. Be rich
   d. Be funny

4. What will some turn away from?
   a. Myths
   b. Stories
   c. Truth
   d. Lies

5. What will they turn to?
   a. Gospel
   b. Truth
   c. Myths
   d. Law

6. What has Paul fought?
   a. A good fight
   b. A good race
   c. A good lion
   d. A good bear

7. Who stood with Paul during this time?
   a. Timothy
   b. God
   c. Mark
   d. John

8. Why does Paul want Mark to come?
   a. He's needy
   b. He's useful for service
   c. He's a kind friend
   d. He's a smart man

9. What did Alexander the coppersmith do to Paul?
   a. Taught him
   b. Preached to him
   c. Harmed him
   d. Loved him

10. Those who love Jesus' appearing will receive the crown of _____.
    a. righteousness
    b. truthfulness
    c. cleanliness
    d. helpfulness

Memory Verse

2 Timothy 4:5

"But you, be sober in all things, endure hardship, do the work of an evangelist, fulfill your ministry."

D4Y "Becoming God's Champion" Final Exam

1. Paul is _____for the Gospel.
   a. suffering
   b. singing
   c. playing
   d. waiting

2. What has been entrusted to Timothy?
   a. The religion
   b. The treasure
   c. A promise
   d. The parchment

3. What crown will Paul receive in the future?
   a. righteousness
   b. happiness
   c. purity
   d. jewels

4. What should Timothy not be ashamed of?
   a. Paul's reputation
   b. The testimony of Jesus
   c. His old age
   d. His physical health

5. What spirit has God *not* given us?
   a. Joy
   b. Peace
   c. Timidity
   d. Love

6. Where do we get our power from?
   a. The sun
   b. The Holy Spirit
   c. Our friends
   d. Our education

7. What did Paul instruct Timothy to do with the standard of sound words?
   a. Forget them
   b. Ignore them
   c. Retain them
   d. Change them

8. Who enables us to guard the treasure?
   a. The Holy Spirit
   b. Paul
   c. Parents
   d. Friends

9. Faithful men will be able to _____others.
   a. love
   b. help
   c. teach
   d. meet

10. How is Timothy to suffer hardship with Paul?
    a. Like a good soldier of Christ
    b. Like a friend
    c. Like a teacher
    d. Like a parent

11. Salvation is in WHOM?
    a. Teachers
    b. Judges
    c. Christ Jesus
    d. Preachers

12. What will we do with Jesus for 1000 years?
    a. Hunt
    b. Reign
    c. Eat
    d. Fish

13. What does an *unbeliever* do with Christ?
    a. Deny Him
    b. Love Him
    c. Praise Him
    d. Serve Him

14. How is Timothy to present himself to God?
    a. Dirty
    b. Approved
    c. Lukewarm
    d. Faithless

D4Y "Becoming God's Champion" Final Exam

15. We are to be vessels of _____.
    a. Truth
    b. Cleanness
    c. Honor
    d. Works

16. The believer is to abstain from _____.
    a. wickedness
    b. Truth
    c. Peace
    d. Kindness

17. How should children be toward their parents?
    a. Rebellious
    b. Obedient
    c. Indifferent
    d. Angry

18. What will God do if we confess our sins?
    a. Be happy
    b. Help us
    c. Forgive us
    d. Bless us

19. What do unfaithful men do with the truth?
    a. Oppose it
    b. Love it
    c. Accept it
    d. Nothing

20. What did God do for Paul?
    a. Forgot him
    b. Left him alone
    c. Rescued him
    d. Discouraged him

21. Who will judge the living and the dead?
    a. Jesus
    b. Moses
    c. Abraham
    d. Mark

22. What is Timothy charged to do with the Word?
    a. Rewrite it
    b. Preach it
    c. Hide it
    d. Ignore it

23. What will unbelievers turn to?
    a. Truth
    b. Law
    c. Myths
    d. Gospel

24. What has Paul fought?
    a. A good race
    b. A good lion
    c. A good bear
    d. A good Fight

25. Those who love Jesus' appearing will receive the crown of _____.
    a. righteousness
    b. truthfulness
    c. cleanliness
    d. helpfulness

Quiz Answer Key

Week 1	Week 2	Week 3	Week 4	Week 5	Week 6
1. b	1. a	1. a	1. a	1. a	1. a
2. c	2. b	2. c	2. b	2. b	2. b
3. a	3. b	3. b	3. c	3. b	3. b
4. a	4. c	4. c	4. a	4. c	4. c
5. b	5. a	5. a	5. c	5. a	5. c
6. c	6. c	6. c	6. a	6. c	6. a
7. a	7. a	7. a	7. b	7. a	7. b
8. b	8. c	8. b	8. c	8. c	8. b
9. c	9. a	9. c	9. a	9. a	9. c
10. b	10. c	10. c	10. c	10. b	10. a

Final Answer Key

1. a	14. b
2. b	15. c
3. a	16. a
4. b	17. b
5. c	18. c
6. b	19. a
7. c	20. c
8. a	21. a
9. c	22. b
10. a	23. c
11. c	24. d
12. b	25. a
13. a	

Optional Games

The Matching Game

You need at least ten questions and answers from the lesson you are studying.

Type the answers on a sheet of paper. Make two sets of answers and cut the answers into individual strips and place each set of answers in an envelope.

Divide your class into two teams. Pick a student from each team and have them come up and stand in front of you, opposite each other (back to back) in the middle of the room. On each side of the room you have taken the answers out of each envelope and mixed them up and placed them in two piles on the floor.

You ask a question and tap the two students in front of you and say "Go." They have to run from you to their side of the room and look for the correct answer to the question you just asked in their pile. If they bring you an incorrect answer, tell them, "Wrong, try again" and they race back again to find the correct answer. The first one to race back to you and bring you the correct answer gets 100 points for their team. You continue to do this until you have answered all your questions and the team with the most points wins.

Optional Games

M&M® Draw

You will need a bag of M&M®s. Empty them into a container you can't see through. Write the point values for the M&M®s on a white board for all the kids to see. I choose point values depending on how many there are of each color—the more there are of a color the lower the point value.

Brown: 100 points

Red: 200 points

Yellow: 300 points

Green: 400 points

Blue: 500 points

Orange: 600 points

Divide the kids into two teams and ask a question from the lesson or book you are studying. If the kid you pick from the first team answers the question correctly, he or she closes their eyes and picks an M&M® from the container. Once they have chosen a color, they get to eat the candy and you record the points they won on the board for their team. If they miss the question, the other team gets to steal the question and draw the M&M®; then it's that team's turn to answer a question. The team with the most points wins.

Reward them with a small piece of candy or a privilege.

If you are working with one student you can still play the game by asking the questions and letting the child answer and draw an M&M® if he/she answers correctly. Tell them if they get to a certain number of points they will receive a reward or privilege.

Optional Games

5W and H Game

Things you need:
- A game board. I use a project board from a school supply store. To set up your board, you need to make 5 category labels WHO, WHAT, WHEN/HOW, WHERE and WHY and place them on your board. (See diagram below.)
- You need five index cards for each category labeled with 100, 200, 300, 400 and 500 points. After labeling your cards with point values, you can laminate your cards to make them last longer and then place a small piece of Velcro on the blank side of the card.
- Put the other part of your Velcro on your game board, five pieces under each category and stick your points on your board.
- You also need to make a question sheet using questions from the book you are studying. Label each question in each category, 100 points for the easiest question, next 200 points, 300 points, 400 points and 500 points for the hardest question.

To play 5W and H Game:
- This game is played like "Jeopardy." Divide your class into two teams
- The team to go second always gets the last question.
- A kid on the team that goes first raises their hand and tells you what category and what point value they want to try and answer a question. As an example a child may say, "I want 'Why' for 500 points." Then you need to read a question on your sheet under the "Why" category for 500 points. If the question is answered correctly then that child has 500 points recorded for his/her team and it's the next team's turn. If the child gives a wrong answer then the other team may try and answer it correctly for the 500 points and then it is their turn to pick a category and a question.
- Alternate with the two teams until you run out of questions or time is up. Make sure that the team who went second gets the last question. Whoever has the most points wins the game.

WHO	WHAT	WHEN/HOW	WHERE	WHY
100	100	100	100	100
200	200	200	200	200
300	300	300	300	300
400	400	400	400	400
500	500	500	500	500

Learn how

you can be involved in "Establishing People in God's Word" at **precept.org/connect**

 Precept.org/connect

Use your smartphone to get connected to Precept's ministry initiatives!
Precept.org/connect

Precept Online Community

provides support, training opportunities, and exclusive resources to help
Bible study leaders and students.

 Precept.org/POC

Use your smartphone to connect to Precept Online Community! **Precept.org/POC**

 Join The Discover 4 Yourself Inductive Bible Studies for Kids! Group in Precept Online Community

CPSIA information can be obtained
at www.ICGtesting.com
Printed in the USA
BVOW10s2056300616

453940BV00007B/1/P